Two Dogmas of Philosophy
and Other Essays
in the
Philosophy of Philosophy

Also by DENNIS A. ROHATYN:

Naturalism and Deontology: An Essay on the Problems of Ethics

Two Dogmas
of Philosophy
and Other Essays
in the
Philosophy of Philosophy

Dennis A. Rohatyn

Rutherford • Madison • Teaneck
Fairleigh Dickinson University Press

London: Associated University Presses

© 1977 by Associated University Presses, Inc.

Associated University Presses, Inc.
Cranbury, New Jersey 08512

Associated University Presses
Magdalen House
136-148 Tooley Street
London SE1 2TT, England

Library of Congress Cataloging in Publication Data

Rohatyn, Dennis A.
Two dogmas of philosophy and other essays in the philosophy
of philosophy.

Bibliography: p.
Includes index.
CONTENTS: Two dogmas of philosophy.—Understanding
philosophy.—Philosophic utterances: an "existential" theory.—
Kierkegaard and his critics. [etc.]
1. Philosophy—Addresses, essays, lectures. 2. Kierkegaard,
Søren Aabye, 1813-1855—Addresses, essays, lectures. 3.
Nietzsche, Friedrich Wilhelm, 1844-1900—Addresses, essays, lec-
tures. I. Title.
B53.R63 1976   100   75-63
ISBN 0-8386-1673-9

163719

PRINTED IN THE UNITED STATES OF AMERICA

For Dan,

who arranged for my "escape" from Luxembourg

Contents

Preface

The essays contained in this volume represent the fruits of several years' reflective labor concerning what philosophy is and is not, and how to go about studying it. Their intent is frankly programmatic and methodological, and their orientation is, to be equally candid, historical, in a sense that the volume itself makes progressively clear. I have not hesitated to address myself to prevailing shibboleths in philosophy, and to speculate on how they might be supplanted by better ones. I have conceived of philosophy throughout this book as more akin to a standard of life than a scientific discipline; in this respect my views are certainly idiosyncratic, but I at least have attempted to present reasons and arguments that I think cogent in bucking manfully the prevailing orthodoxies and resisting the contemporary winds of fashion.

I have learned much from reading and even more from my teachers. If pressed to name one, I should immediately say that Sir Isaiah Berlin has been more influential than any other single source in compelling me to think and rethink my assumptions, and indeed to discover and evaluate the presuppositions governing my own view of the philosophic enterprise. Other sources are too numerous to mention, let alone thank for all the stimulus they have imparted. It goes without saying that the responsibility for the ideas presented here is strictly and entirely my own.

Acknowledgments

I would like to thank the following for permission to reprint copyrighted material:

A. & C. Black Ltd for permission to quote from Søren Kierkegaard, *Johannes Climacus; or, De Omnibus Dubitandum Est, and A Sermon*, translated by T. H. Croxall.

Professor Brand Blanshard for permission to quote from his "Kierkegaard on Faith," *The Personalist* 49 (1968).

Professor Paul Edwards for permission to quote from his "Kierkegaard and the 'Truth' of Christianity," *Philosophy* 46 (1971).

The Personalist for permission to quote from Brand Blanshard, "Kierkegaard on Faith," *The Personalist* 49 (1968): 5-23.

Philosophy for permission to quote from Paul Edwards, "Kierkegaard and the 'Truth' of Christianity," *Philosophy* 46 (1971): 89-108.

Stanford University Press for permission to quote from Søren Kierkegaard, *Johannes Climacus; or, De Omnibus Dubitandum Est, and A Sermon*, translated by T. H. Croxall.

Universitas for permission to reprint, with revisions, my "Who Is Nietzsche's Overman?", *Universitas* 4 (1974): 31-45.

Two Dogmas of Philosophy
and Other Essays
in the
Philosophy of Philosophy

1
Two Dogmas of Philosophy

P hilosophy is a lot like the weather. Everyone talks about it, but few are impelled to do anything to improve it. I frankly avow that my purpose here is to add to the list of complaints that have been lodged against the contemporary philosophical scene, especially in the English-speaking world. If my remarks do make a constructive contribution, it will be indirectly.

Nonetheless, the criticisms I am about to make are of importance if we wish to understand the methodology of much contemporary thought, as well as the mentality that lies behind it. For this reason I think them worth airing.

My title is a paraphrase of a famous article by Quine; but

the dogmas I want to uncover have nothing to do with the ones he unearthed. In speaking of "dogmas" I wish to call attention to the status that certain doctrines or tenets seem to me to enjoy in some philosophic circles at present, and to suggest reasons why they should be called into question. My inquiry is therefore a logical preliminary to any philosophic undertaking, and may therefore justly be characterized as "metaphilosophical" in scope. But this term should not be misleading; I do not intend that metaphilosophical researches should be a substitute for the generation of philosophical ideas themselves, nor do I imply that "metaphilosophy" stands on any safer or firmer ground than does philosophy itself, or indeed that it is anything divorced or distinct from philosophic reflection. In being about philosophy, metaphilosophy is simply an extension, and therefore an enrichment, of the subject.

Briefly, the two dogmas I have in mind are as follows: (1) philosophy is a branch of knowledge, and (2) the essence of philosophy lies in reasoned argument. These two dogmas are related, and not by accident, but each figures prominently in independently formulated discussions of what philosophy is about. In challenging each of these two dogmas, I am far from claiming that no good case can be made for the pursuit of philosophy as a worthwhile endeavor. Part of what I am going to say is that the value of philosophic study does not have to depend on upholding either of the principles I have just stated. I am also quite far from an authoritative pronouncement that neither doctrine is in any way tenable—for that would be dogmatism, and I want to eschew dogmatism all around, not merely insofar as it concerns what other people maintain. Mine shall be a plea for tolerance, even compassion, on the part of philosophers for one another—a quality, or call it a virtue, that I find much lacking today, and at the same time one that is badly needed.

The account I am about to launch may strike some people as impressionistic. So be it. While I have tried to avoid pedantry, I will document, by quotation or example or simply reference, wherever I think it significant or appropriate to do so. One may judge for himself whether the portrait I am about to paint is accurate, a faithful likeness.

A. *Philosophy as a branch of knowledge.* For some time now—I mean upwards of two millennia—philosophy has been trivially as well as etymologically described as "love of wisdom." But if the term *wisdom* means anything, it means an ability to get along in life without knowledge, or without objective certainty, and to endure the vicissitudes of fortune accordingly, and preferably, with calm. Moreover, as Plato observes, we love those things we lack; those which we already possess we desire only to perpetuate or hold in our keep. Thus love of wisdom amounts to love for something we lack, and something that is at best a knowledge surrogate. Although I have only sketched the implications of the phrase "love of wisdom," a further exploration of what the term "philosophy" means, taken in this spirit, would, I believe, bear my contentions out, and besides that, would enjoy some definite merits as a philosophical (and ethical) position in its own right.

But is philosophy's stature as "love of wisdom" more of a curse than a blessing? Judging from the activity of philosophers in the Western tradition, this would seem to be the case. Time and time again they have attempted to defy the limitations that the subject would seem to impose on them. This may have begun, as philosophy itself did, with the pre-Socratics. Time was when the Burnet interpretation of the early Ionians was sacrosanct. Today, thanks to the work of such scholars as Rohde, Harrison, Cornford, and more recently, Guthrie, this is no longer the case. But while the "pre-Sophistic" thinkers, as Cleve calls them, may have had a strong "religious" or "mystical" bent, there can be no doubt that a strong part of their interest and enthusiasm lay in the direction of what are now called the physical or natural sciences. This has been amply illustrated by such writers as Sambursky, Popper, Kirk, Sarton, and Thorndike.

I do not, however, need to retreat into the fog of pre-Socratic philosophic history, surrounded as it is by legend and unreliable reports, in order to trace a clear pattern of philosophical alliance with science. In Plato, problems of interpretation of the dialogues notwithstanding, we find a definite longing to elevate philosophy to the status of knowledge, with mathematics as the familiar metaphor or parallel, and sometimes as the method of approaching this goal. Plato's *Meno, Republic* VI and VII, *Timaeus,* and other dialogues all bear witness to the yearning to make of philosophy a science, indeed an exact science.

Aristotle inherits this mantle uncritically. It is often said that the metaphor changes from mathematics to biology (as in *De Anima,* or *Metaphysics* Theta), but this is only partly true, especially in view of the *Organon;* both Aristotle's pioneering work in formal logic and semantics, and his discussion of *episteme* in the *Posterior Analytics,* suggest that his commitment to philosophy as (ideally) deductive reasoning with theorematic fruits runs every bit as deep as Plato's.

Although the Alexandrian and later Hellenistic periods are sometimes looked down upon as ones of intellectual infertility, it suffices to note that here the rise of speculative metaphysics, in the form of Neoplatonism, and the work, about which we still know altogether too little, of the Stoic logicians, both support the thesis that philosophy was viewed during this era, even if intermittently, as supplying definite principles pretending to describe "reality" as well as to guide conduct or establish norms of thought and behavior.

In the medieval period, foolish as it is to attempt a

sweeping delineation, there can be no doubt that philosophy, even in its oft-misunderstood ancillary role, was meant to perform the same functions I have just mentioned. No one can read the work of a competent historian such as Gilson[1] without concluding that, whatever divided medieval thinkers from one another by virtue of era, geography, and temperament, they were, at least until the time of Cusanus, more or less united in their confidence that philosophy could handle the ontological tasks and responsibilities assigned to it, which, in retrospect, were both enormous and (consequently) unsupportable.

After the so-called "break-up of the medieval synthesis" had occurred, something strange happened: philosophers rededicated themselves to finding the fount of knowledge. But the manner in which they presumed to discover it, or the results of their separate labors, were no longer uniform. For Descartes, as for Plato before him, the model of knowledge was mathematics; for Bacon, it was the collection of information. Concurrently, modern science as we know it was pioneered, and was not without its effect on inspired imitators, such as Leibniz and Spinoza, as well as slavish ones, such as Hobbes, whose best work was done in spite, not because, of his uncomprehending admiration for what was then the novelty of scientific achievement.

After the much-heralded "destruction of natural theology" by Hume and Kant, one might be forgiven for expecting that the drive to make philosophy into a branch of settled knowledge would cease. But Kant himself was too perceptive to believe in the effect of his own monumental work; as he trenchantly puts it, "the human mind would no sooner give up metaphysical researches than it would prefer to stop breathing in order to avoid inhaling impurities" (*Prolegomena,* after para. 60). The "resuscitation" of philosophy

1. E. Gilson, *A History of Christian Philosophy in the Middle Ages* (New York: Random House, 1955), *passim.*

began anew with Hegel. Note that, for reasons best known to themselves, both Hegel and his phenomenological descendant of a century later, Husserl, chose to call the product of their reflections *Wissenschaft*. Their methods, let alone results, had very little in common with one another, and still less with Plato, or with Descartes. They had no connection whatsoever with science in the sense of modern (and by this I do not mean contemporary, but only seventeenth- through nineteenth-century) physics, biology, or chemistry.

At the same time, there were philosophers who did counsel their peers to remain attuned to the work of their scientific colleagues. Unfortunately, these men often went beyond their own self-imposed restraints: Comte's Religious Humanism and Spencer's Social Darwinism are two good examples of untrammeled, even wild extrapolations that claimed scientific status but had no right even to suggest science as a partner in their respective enterprises. Meanwhile, philosophers who remained "sober," such as J. S. Mill, were quickly discarded because of advances, especially in logic, that made their work obsolete or useless. (It is perhaps only because Mill achieved fame in ethics and social philosophy that his outworn statements on truth-criteria, the mind-body problem, the External World Dilemma, remain staples in the diet of anthologies, while, curiously, his contribution to inductive logic is never studied in its own right, but is regarded as authoritative in textbooks, even though Mill's Methods are entirely unoriginal with Mill, being "honestly plagiarized" from a much earlier writer).

To move this discussion rapidly into our own century, we encounter yet another anomaly: while continental philosophy has not given up its pretentious and pompous ways, it rarely deigns to call itself science, perhaps because this term (or its corollary, *technology*) has become offensive in certain quarters; on the other hand, Viennese positivism, transplanted into Great Britain and the United States and lingering on as a lukewarm brand of "logical empiricism," invokes science at every turn, not only with regard to such supposedly dead issues as the Verifiability Criterion, but also in the methods, techniques, and above all the interests of its leading practitioners and spiritual children, Hempel and the late Carnap being the most notable instances.

That there have been, and currently are, other movements, and other philosophers, I should never care to deny. But if one were to make a list of those great figures of our own time who have been under the stimulus of either logic or one of the empirical sciences, one would have to include Russell, Dewey, Wittgenstein, Whitehead, Cassirer, and even Bergson; and certainly Jaspers. The exceptions, such as Moore, Heidegger, and Sartre, are just that; for what it is worth, they are outnumbered, and therefore are mavericks, rather than indicative of trends.

Those who have followed my brief survey of the course of philosophic thought thus far are undoubtedly expecting some sort of philosophic, or unphilosophic, diatribe against science as the next step in the endeavor. Far from it. Instead, I wish to raise the following question: granted that we consistently come across links between philosophy and some conception of science, or whatever prevailing model of knowledge may be appropriated as ultimate arbiter, why is it that after each shift of fashion, or upon each "defeat" suffered by a once-prevalent world view, (some) philosophers attempt with renewed vigor to set up the same old standard, albeit slightly or grossly modified, but usually employing the same or very similar terminology?

More simply, what I am asking is this: what is the motivation for this philosophic drive toward knowledge, or scientific status? I realize that this is not a question susceptible to a valid, general answer; it is perhaps one that can only be asked intelligibly for individual cases, in which context it becomes purely biographical or psychological. But I think it is a question important to ask, if only because history demonstrates that the program that philosophy sometimes sets up for itself inevitably flounders. Perhaps, as certain "linguistic" philosophers intimate, we should after all limit our sights and be more modest in our aims than our predecessors have seen fit to be, especially because philosophy finds itself, as never before, circumscribed by the very subjects that were once called philosophy but are now "independent" in both method and content: astronomy, to name one; behavioral psychology for another. (This is not to say that these fields lack philosophical presuppositions, but they do not conceive it as part of their task to elicit them, whereas philosophy does—not only for astronomy or psychology, but also reflexively).

Perhaps, too, if they learn not to set impossible goals for themselves, philosophers will not be so desperately unhappy, so Faustian in the moods they sometimes petulantly display before themselves and others. But such a "therapeutic" by-product I would in any event regard as only a secondary benefit.

In attempting to deal with this problem, I think it only fair to fall back upon one piece of earlier research on the same topic. I am speaking of Nietzsche. Nietzsche is not merely the first, but the only major philosopher even to raise the kind of issues I am concerned with here. As everyone will remember, he lampooned the "will to truth" as a "philosopher's prejudice" (*Beyond Good and Evil*, 1-2, 43-44). What could be more galling? He goes on to stick the needle in further: ". . .no one has yet been sufficiently truthful about the nature of 'truthfulness.' " (*ibid.*, 177). What Nietzsche envisioned, it seems to me, is a *sociology of philosophy*. I do not mean the kind of thing that Naess does—the distribution of questionnaires to freshmen students asking them what they think of the *cogito*, before and after their professors have explained it to them, with a statistical tabulation of the responses. What I mean is an investigation into the qualities of the philosophic outlook, both past and contemporaneous. Since the philosophic attachment to science is, as I have just tried to show, a major feature in any philosophic epoch, it stands to reason that a "scientific" approach to the sociology of philosophy will not do. It will be biased rather than detached; it will be, in the fashionable lingo of exhortative bureaucrats, part of the problem instead of a means to its solution. (I also think that the results it exhibits will be superficial and uninteresting; if proof is needed, one may turn to the discipline of sociology itself. Long after the computerized study of social phenomena is buried, people will still be reading, and with profit, the works of "armchair moralists" such as Riesman, Goodman, Whyte, Berger and others who do not seek to evade the problem of surreptitious value commitments in the social sciences by drowning themselves and their audience in a sea of numbers. But this is a personal opinion, and constitutes a digression from my main theme).

Since the kind of critique in which Nietzsche engaged has never been picked up or developed by anyone, even when its validity was appreciated, it is moot to wonder just how one might properly go about elaborating a sociology of philosophy for today. Taste requires that we exclude the sort of open gossip that Diogenes Laertius exudes, and concentrate on the issues; but beyond that, there are no immediately available guidelines.

The "will to truth" cannot be far removed from either the Deweyan "quest for certainty," or what I have loosely called the drive for knowledge; the differences are matters of vocabulary only, and do not conceal or reveal any deep, nonsemantic differences between and among the various possible formulations. But there is one idea that should be added, in order to make the picture more comprehensive. It seems to me that, above all, philosophers (with the exception of Nietzsche) have been concerned to make philosophy *respectable*. I think this is as true today as it was in Athens, or Rome, or in Koenigsberg. Philosophy has *always* been a "scandal": a scandal to others, as symbolized by the pestiferous, gadfly approach of a Socrates, and a scandal to itself, in that it has never—and I know this is a sweeping, albeit negative claim—been able to provide one item that might definitively be counted as knowledge, or a step in that direction. A sustained defense of this point is made in a recent, brilliant article by Richard Taylor. To quote from a single passage:

> Almost any philosopher knows. . .that Socrates died in 399 BC, that he taught Plato, believed in the immortality of the soul. . .a philosopher can explain what pragmatism is, is likely to know Santayana's theories of essences, and can usually give some account of Kant's transcendental aesthetic. But none of this is philosophical knowledge. . .just as such knowledge (about music or poetry) fails to make one a musician or a poet, so likewise the knowledge about philosophy, however great, does not make one a philosopher.[2]

While I happen to feel that Taylor's judgment on the value of historical erudition is harsh, not least because it presupposes that well-informed and critical philosophical skill cannot add anything to it, I do agree with him that there is nothing in philosophy that can be counted as "progress," except in the sense of progressive enrichment of the subject by the appearance of additional works, espousing new (or reworking old) points of view, and therefore multiplying an already bewildering, but comforting, diversity.

2. R. Taylor, "Dare to be Wise," *Review of Metaphysics* 21 (1967-68): 619.

The mention of Socrates provokes me to recall his pertinent profession of ignorance, his insistence that the only thing he knew was that he did not know anything (else).[3] This is neither false modesty nor a predisposition for the paradoxical; even within the context of the Platonic dialogues, it is more truthful than we may care to admit or realize. After all, it is in the *Parmenides* that Plato finds his own Theory of Ideas, placed in the mouth of the "young" Socrates, decisively attacked and refuted; and it is in the mid- to late-period, but nonetheless aporetic, *Theaetetus*, that we "learn" that "knowledge" cannot be successfully defined. But, to pose a typically Socratic question, if "knowledge" cannot be successfully defined, then how can we even talk about instantiations thereof? Keeping in mind that in the area of epistemology philosophy has really not advanced one whit beyond the subtleties of the *Theaetetus*, we are compelled to wonder what right we have to employ the term "knowledge" at all, whether in philosophy, in the sciences—which still depend upon a philosophic reconstruction of their methods, doctrines, and overall procedure—or even in a scholarly presentation such as this? These are questions that many philosophers have no doubt asked themselves privately, but few have dared to confess their uncertainties in public, or for the benefit of posterity. (Perhaps this is why, for all his unjust vilification of Socrates, Nietzsche found himself irresistibly attracted to the Socratic *daimon*, as to no other model of philosophizing. But that is another matter).

The world has always found it difficult to live with philosophy, but it is equally true that philosophers have always found it difficult to live among themselves. Since knowledge in philosophy (as opposed to knowledge about, or of philosophy) is a mirage, it is easy to see why tensions

3. Discussed by Taylor, "Dare to be Wise," p. 616.

arise from within the community itself. Since knowledge is an illusion, quacks and other dubious practitioners have an easy time obtaining a license. In Plato's day the Sophists were the leading group of pseudo-philosophers, and is it any wonder that Socrates, even in retrospect, is sometimes mistakenly labeled as one of them? In later times it was the alchemist. According to Schopenhauer (and partially echoed by Russell and Broad), it was Hegel. And even today, the plain man has a hard time distinguishing between philosophy as cultivated in the universities, and such things as astrology, scientology, or even palm-reading. If you doubt my words, check any edition of the Manhattan Yellow Pages: you will find under "Metaphysician" one or two entries for any given recent year. (Jacques Barzun once reported that he was tempted to actually consult such a doctor, but evidently good sense got the better of him). In such a carnival atmosphere, is it surprising that philosophy generates such enormous intramural frictions, and that (periodically) philosophers call for the exclusion of other members of the profession from the ranks—witness Carnap's denigration of Heidegger, or Heidegger's of Cassirer, and so on? With the emergence of a professionalized, academic class of philosophers, in close contact with one another's thoughts and meeting regularly throughout the world for interchange of ideas, it is equally unastonishing that philosophers should by this time have banded together in closed cliques—analysts on one side, phenomenologists on another; pragmatists here, and existentialists there; and hostile subdivisions within these unarmed camps, aiming verbal barrages at one another.

If someone had a strategy for ruining philosophy, it could not have been better planned than what philosophers have done by dividing themselves into groups of mutually opposed intellectual forces. After all, the worldwide philosophic community is relatively small to begin with.

There is no advantage in carrying on in a spirit of warfare when philosophy is already badly "outnumbered" by those who do not see any valid contribution coming from anywhere inside it. Philosophy is not just dying or dead, as some prognosticators of doom, such as Lewis Feuer, may indicate; it is killing itself, but the suicide is producing more grief than any of the problems that have brought it on could possibly muster.

I am not about to call for a moratorium on disagreement, nor am I ready to plead for unity in philosophy. On the contrary, I am as distrustful of unity as I am of the apparent or surface discord in philosophy that I have just outlined. Underneath all that, philosophers remain unchanged; almost to a man they believe that philosophy yields knowledge. They do not agree, as the medievals did, on what knowledge is or on what its object or referent is; but each is sublimely certain that he, singly or in collaboration with colleagues who are of a like persuasion, has arrived at what Nietzsche mockingly called the Truth, and that therefore what he and his confrères are doing is supremely worthwhile—while everyone else be damned. It was left for Tarski to discern this attitude, many years ago; but only Dewey seems to have noticed (and approved of) the Tarskian assessment.[4] I might add, as Nietzsche would emphasize, that Truth is a contagious disease infecting all the domains of scholarship, so that philosophy is not unique in succumbing to it. But I must leave scholars in other fields to attend to cleaning out their own Augean stables for themselves, without intruding on their province.

Even followers of the ripe philosophy of Wittgenstein, who presumably should know better, are often guilty of

4. A. Tarski, "The Semantic Conception of Truth, and the Foundations of Semantics," *Philosophy and Phenomenological Research* 4 (1944-45): 345; reprinted in L. Linsky, ed., *Semantics and the Philosophy of Language* (Urbana, Ill.: University of Illinois Press, 1952), p. 17; quoted and discussed in John Dewey and Arthur F. Bentley, *Knowing and the Known* (Boston: Beacon Press, 1949), p. 32.

writing as though in perfect accord with tradition, instead of fostering a genuine departure therefrom. The most refreshing (and perhaps only eminent) exception is found in the work of O.K. Bouwsma;[5] the rest are closet rebels, metaphysicians in ordinary language clothing.

Dewey is one philosopher who does not overestimate the potential of philosophy, either for examining phenomena in the world, or for issuing moral pronouncements, tied to and derivative from a comprehensive metaphysical thesis. But Dewey's views, whether in 1896 or during the 1930s, have always been harnessed, and rather servilely at that, to one sophisticated version of scientific naturalism.[6] Hence the only philosopher whom I know of who is not committed to any extra-philosophic discipline for the source of his inspiration is Austin. And, reading Austin, it is instructive to note how disenchanted he can sometimes get with his own subject—a subject that he has often been accused of trimming down to an unpalatable narrowness, too. Participating in a colloquium in 1958, Austin, searching for an illuminating description of philosophy, settled upon the following characterization:

> [philosophy is] more like the surface of the sun—a pretty fair mess. You disentangle yourself as best you can with the means you have at hand. . .philosophy. . .deals with what's left over, all the problems that remain still insoluble, after all the other recognized methods have been tried. It's the dumping ground for all the leftovers from other sciences, where everything turns up which we don't know quite how to take. As soon as someone discovers a respectable and reliable method of handling

5. O. K. Bouwsma, *Philosophical Essays* (Lincoln, Neb.: University of Nebraska Press, 1965), *passim*.

6. See esp. John Dewey, *The Quest for Certainty*, new ed. (New York: Capricorn Books, 1960), p. 273, on the direction that the natural sciences are asked to give to attempts to establish norms for human action; and also *Experience and Nature*, 2d ed. (Chicago: Open Court, 1929), *passim*.

some portion of these residual problems, a new science is set up, which tends to break away from philosophy.[7]

And, as William James, who saw philosophy from the dual vantage-point of moralist and empirical psychologist, might have added, the foregoing pattern of development (which James astutely labeled as philosophy's supplying "grist" for the scientific mill) leaves philosophy in a woeful state of distress. The "queen of the sciences" is left to complain dyspeptically about her desertion by former suitors, about being left to rest on her past laurels—surely a decadent posture. But decadence is better than nothing, and so philosophers will lose no time in pointing out that philosophy once embraced all of the things to which Austin alludes, and has therefore not only been productive, but has earned the undying gratitude of mankind, instead of the heaps of scorn to which it has frequently been (mis-) treated. But, in the words of the time-honored rebuttal to this recitation of past accomplishment: what has philosophy done for us lately? Nothing? Good; then let us dispense with philosophy, forthwith!

As I have mentioned, few philosophers, because of their vested interest, have the courage to raise such questions, or, like Austin, to propose what I earlier referred to as a modest alternative course. And, if philosophers find it difficult to live together in anything resembling "philosophic" harmony, still more trying is it for individual philosophers to live with themselves, to face up to the "bankruptcy" of their own discipline, as Nietzsche was able to do. Then again, Nietzsche went mad, which is even more eloquent tes-

7. J. L. Austin, "Performative-Constative," trans. G. J. Warnock, in C. E. Caton, ed., *Philosophy and Ordinary Language* (Urbana, Ill.; University of Illinois Press, 1963), p. 42. Cf. "Ifs and Cans," reprinted in *Philosophical Papers*, 2d ed., ed. J. O. Urmson and G. J. Warnock (Oxford: Clarendon Press, 1970), p. 232, on how to "get rid of philosophy" by turning 'linguistic analysis' into a science and so "kicking it [philosophy] upstairs."

timony as to what happens to people who interrogate themselves as relentlessly as Nietzsche—or a Socrates, who drove his community to madness, and so, by diverse means, arrived at the same untoward end as Nietzsche. It should be reasonably clear now why philosophers are from time to time impelled by an urge to make philosophy respectable, or, to use the economic metaphor, solvent, as it has never been heretofore. Can it be done? We have strong inductive evidence, gleaned from past failures, to support the contrary thesis, and while this is not sufficient to deter an apriorist, let alone a representative of the kind of timeless rational speculation on God, freedom, and immortality that Kant sees as forever recurrent in the human intellect, it should at least give us pause. Unless, of course, we happen to believe that somebody before us has already discovered (or created, as the case may be) the Truth, or reached the Absolute—in which case, again, there is nothing left for philosophy to do but disband. And yet I take it that this result would be undesirable, if only because the Truth needs to be rearticulated and reiterated. This is what is sometimes called "education," or at least the transmission of past ideas into the present milieu. Whether one thinks that this is an overdone or an underemphasized aspect of education, I have yet to hear anyone who would object stridently to it altogether.

So we are bound to conclude that while St. Thomas Aquinas or perhaps Gilbert Ryle may have uttered the Last Word in philosophy some time ago, there is still a need to keep a few philosophers—as distinguished from what Taylor would consider mere antiquarians—around for an indefinite while, to act as spokesmen on behalf of the Truth.

But if this be the case, then we must consent to the proposition, harmless on its face, that in some sense the work of philosophy, even if it is only of the missionary and proselytizing kind, is as yet, and perhaps perpetually, unfinished. But if the job philosophy has to do is unfinished, a suspicion must linger on that it is unfinished in the more significant sense of not yet having arrived at the summit, of not having brought its project of universal knowledge (or metaphysics by any other name) to completion and fulfillment. When we add the observation that in fact the devotees of a variety of philosophical standpoints are currently found, each claiming either exclusive monopoly on the Truth, or at least a patent on access to it, and with no one of these positions having gained either the consensus among the plurality, or better still the majority, of fellow-laborers, or even the kind of artificial ascendancy that internal politics and episodes in taste and fashion may dictate, then the problematic of contemporary philosophy in all of its vain glory is thrown into relief.

To put it more economically: does philosophy have a future, as philosophy, and not merely as a tired rehash of well-entrenched modes of perceiving things and events and other people, of seeing ourselves against that vast background of cosmos and society? If it does—and no philosopher hopes, whatever he may profess, that it does not—then the arrogance of even a limited claim to finality must be the spur to Humean skepticism, even at the considerable risk of having to face "nihilism," or some less-hysterical-sounding equivalent, as a logical consequence of entertaining our own methodic doubt; doubt not of the existence of the world around us, but of the dubiously founded interpretations of it offered by philosophers, no matter how great or how prestigious.

This brings me by slow turns to my second point, namely, the predominant contemporary view of philosophy, which sees for it, and in it, all a matter of technique and none of substance, without realizing that the recommended technique itself betrays a philosophic position, one with certain severe drawbacks.

B. *Philosophy as argument.* In recent years philosophers have become more preoccupied with the relation between philosophy and rhetoric than at any time since the days of itinerant orators, those journeymen debators who plied their trade, as Cicero and St. Augustine, respectively, recount for us, in various cities of Europe, Asia, and Africa. There is now a journal devoted to philosophy and rhetoric, as well as some distinguished books on the subject, by Johnstone, Perelman, and others. But if philosophic argument and rhetorical appeals are now receiving the stress they deserve, a widespread, very doctrinaire attitude toward the role of argument in philosophy is not. I am afraid that the time has come to expose and criticize this (mis)conception.

In this regard, I consider some recent statements by Morris Weitz to be paradigmatic. He writes that by definition philosophy contains a "minimum standard" of "argument as well as assertion."[8] Alasdair Macintyre makes much the same case against Marcuse, charging that Marcuse has failed to live up to the philosophic requirement that a position be established, not merely pronounced.[9] And Antony Flew contrasts philosophy conceived as argument—as reasoned debate, the making explicit of tacit assumptions, and skill in drawing deductive conclusions from a nonenthymematic premise-set—with what he calls a "non-argumentative vision of the world," which Flew refuses to honor by calling it philosophy.[10]

Weitz laments the fact that allegedly a large number of philosophers, including Albert Hofstadter, one of whose books Weitz happens to have reviewed, do not share Weitz's view of the obligations entailed by the working

8. M. Weitz, review of A. Hofstadter, *Philosophical Review* 81 (1972): 110-13.

9. A. Macintyre, *Herbert Marcuse: An Exposition and a Polemic* (New York: Viking Press, 1970), pp. 14-15.

10. A. G. N. Flew, *An Introduction to Western Philosophy* (Indianapolis, Ind.: Bobbs-Merrill, 1971), pp. 25-26, 34-38 (esp. p. 36), 477-78, 484.

philosopher. Weitz also writes as though at one time everybody, or nearly so, held the same views that he determines to be appropriate, but that nowadays hell has broken loose, and philosophy has degenerated to the point where it is no longer redeemable. In these respects Weitz goes further than either Macintyre or Flew, whose respective grumblings are neither prolonged, nor quite so polemical, as Weitz's. I do not wish here to cavil with individual philosophers, so I will take the liberty of treating their views cumulatively and not singly. The position taken by any one of the philosophers I have just mentioned is, I think, representative of a trend in philosophy that is itself a late-comer to the philosophical scene but has attracted so many partisans in academic departments as to become, as I see it, the equivalent of gospel. The fact that these three authors write in the same vein is certainly sufficient indication that the viewpoint for which they are such vociferous spokesmen is not in an isolated or embattled corner. Even if the stance that Weitz, Macintyre, and Flew all take were less powerful a force in university philosophy than I am convinced it is, I would feel compelled to offer the following criticisms. These are not meant to constitute a refutation, because that would be to play into the hands of my opponents. They are intended instead as remarks, observations, suggestions, and evaluations of a perspective that has undeniable merits but is one at which I must respectfully demur.

First let us notice that to define philosophy in any way is to enact a piece of legislation. By what right is this invoked? By the perfect right enjoyed by any philosopher, like any other artist, to delimit *for himself* the materials of his craft. This is perfectly legitimate. What is not licit, in my opinion, is the denial of the same freedom to others. Thus we find a James Ross, who defines philosophical theology in such a way as to include the use of modal logic but at the same time to exclude what he vaguely terms "apologetics."[11] This may be fine for Ross, but what does it do but cast a slur on the activity of the self-styled apologist? Any definition will exclude certain possibilities while activating certain others. But it is, to put it mildly, a breach of etiquette to legislate what the field is and is not, for the supposed benefit of others. That such a thing is done at all is an indication that philosophers want to escape from what Austin calls "a pretty fair mess," taking flight and refuge in a haven of their own invention in the hope that they can cajole others into supporting them in their efforts to make philosophy as respectable (and as easy to define) as, say, mechanical engineering.

To put it another way, anyone who tries to tell you what philosophy is or ought to be, and therefore by implication what it is not or should not be, is palming off what Stevenson dubbed a "persuasive definition." It is a mere proposal masquerading as an authoritative pronouncement. Its merits, if any, will be relative to the person who uses the definition for whatever "philosophical" purposes he may envision. There is no such thing as a good (or correct) or a bad (or a wrong) definition of philosophy, except insofar as it enables someone to provide some illuminating comment on any area *he* chooses to work in, or, likewise, insofar as it may prevent that from being accomplished. Definitions—if I may lapse into dogmatism of my own for just a second— are heuristic and operational. I am not saying that there is no such thing as a definitive definition of philosophy; *many* such definitions abound. But they are all bogus, insofar as they are extended to cover (and thereby judge) the work of people besides their perpetrators. I suppose a similar caveat could be filed with regard to the clash between different (not necessarily opposing) philosophical "systems."

11. J. F. Ross, *Philosophical Theology* (Indianapolis, Ind.: Bobbs-Merrill, 1969), esp. pp. 11-12, 14, 16-18, 34, 320-21.

Second, any definition of philosophy should be open to theoretical or other objections. The tone in which the definition of philosophy as (logical or discursive) argument is formulated is not gifted with such liberality, however, no matter where or when it is encountered. It demands assent from its reader as a preliminary to anything else. This puts the definer in an odd position. He may impale himself on the horns of the following dilemma: philosophy equals argument, but you may not argue with my definition (you may only visit another bar). The definition, since it is metaphilosophical, preserves the definer against the charge of contradiction, but he is nonetheless far from immune, since his view of philosophy as argument cannot be said to be thoroughgoing. In an important way, it is only half a loaf. Moreover, because I frankly disbelieve that metaphilosophy is a safe retreat, and therefore disavow for myself any prospect of finality, whether in philosophy or the ancillary disciplines that (as Austin points out) it is forever spawning, I do not see how a definition of philosophy, at any level, and of any type, can be made as smugly as those definitions of philosophy which make it to consist solely and entirely of the process (and result) of reasoned argumentation, would have us accept.

My motto, while admittedly trite, would be "live and let live." Let each man have his own definition of philosophy, and let him apply it to whatever he cares to. But by whose grace is one philosopher permitted to interfere with the designs of another? To avoid the risk of being charged with a rhetorical question, I will answer it flatly: by nobody's. In saying this, I am perhaps admitting that there are "principles" after all. But the fruit of my transcendental methodology is not a specious philosophic doctrine, but simply a rule of fair play; if adhered to, it points to the fulfillment of conditions enabling philosophy to be carried on without antagonisms or a spirit of animosity; hence it is not a logical truth, but a deontological maxim, which, alas, is far more often broken than honored.

There are in addition several strange, not to say incurably disadvantageous, consequences that flow from defining philosophy by way of the skeletal pattern of thought that is said to permeate it. The first and most obvious of these is that philosophy is emptied of content. After all, a sound argument, or for that matter an unsound one, can be found in science, in politics, in religion, in art, or in any other area that fascinates the human mind. Are we to say that all of this is philosophy, and philosophy only? Hardly. What do philosophers talk about? Typically, they concern themselves with such things as perception, deriving "ought" from "is," the ontological proof, the meaning of happiness, the maximization of utility, the mind-body problem, and the like. These are topics; they are distinct from talking about such things as whether or not Mozart wrote all or only part of his *Requiem*, K. 626, or whether the Dodgers will win the pennant this year. But if philosophy is to be defined as simply argument, then it becomes incapable of encompassing *any* of the topics that usually engage philosophic attention. Moreover, since arguments can be and are constructed to show that the Dodgers will (or will not) win the pennant, or to prove that Mozart did (or did not) write the sections that Suessmayr later filled in, why not extend the domain of philosophy to include such predictions and retrodictions, filled in with the appropriate marshaling of evidence to support the respective contentions?

In short, one chief and cogent objection that can be lodged against such a definition as I am here discussing is that it is hopelessly vague, or without any intelligent restrictions. (This is also true of the appealing, Wittgensteinian-inspired, simplistic definition of philosophy as an "activity" that is currently enjoying some vogue. In what respect does this differentiate philosophy from tennis, eating, or sex?) Once restricted (as has not been done), it is no longer the same definition, even in appearance, and it runs into precisely the obstacle I have just set out; given that philosophy equals argument, what prompts the making of the kind of selection of distinct themes to which this ambiguous definition is (meant) to apply? I submit that *any* such selection will in the end be as arbitrary (which is not to say, unfounded) as is the definition, in any of its numerous verbal guises. This defect cannot, I think, be corrected except at the cost of scrapping the original pretensions that accompany it.

As an aside, I should like to note that no question in philosophy today is more frequent—or more irritating—than "what is your philosophy?" When asked by a non-philosopher, sometimes and disparagingly referred to as a "layman," the question provokes the irascible reply "You don't understand what philosophy is about"; or the fashionable "You betray your ignorance on such matters; philosophy is no longer like that, thank goodness." Just to reassure you that I am not inventing dialogue, recall that an Englishman named John Wilson has actually written a series of introductory books in philosophy, in which just such an interchange between omniscient author and ignorant reader is repeatedly conducted.

From within philosophy, however, the question is designed to dredge up on the part of the responder, not some well-thought-out words on the meaning of life (for, as another reviewer, Judith Jarvis Thomson, candidly explains, "most of us [i.e., professional philosophers] genuinely prefer not to be asked any more"[12]), but an affidavit concerning his party affiliation—be it logic and semantics, linguistics, or an even more avant-garde attempt to flee from the painful reality of philosophic disrepute, by pinning one's hopes

---

12. J. J. Thomson, review of R. Taylor, *Philosophical Review* 81 (1972): 113-16.

onto a latter-day science, and attaching oneself, with full "philosophic" weight, thereto.

But the layman's question cannot help but be ignorant, or he would not be (by definition?) a layman, and probably not considered boorish enough to ask. The philosopher who cannot answer it without being snide is betraying more than his impatience with the untutored—like a Callicles or a Polus with Socrates—namely, the fact that when the prevailing spirit is such as to regard philosophy and argument as being coextensive, or interchangeable, not to say synonymous, it is too weak logically to equip philosophers who subscribe to it to *have* a philosophy, or even a set of justifiable interests (as opposed to concentration on something else)—justifiable, in the sense of being recognizably philosophic, and recognizable for a reason, not just by imperious fiat. In this one connection, I am with Weitz, Macintyre, Flew, and the rest; I want reasons for what I am studying, too. (But, unlike those, I am able to live without any assurance of receiving them, precisely because I would be unable to live with myself were I to adopt a dishonest policy; and to my mind, defining philosophy as argument and making that simultaneously one's exclusive province, and a limiting condition for someone else to be designated as a fellow philosopher, is dishonest. Like Hume, I shall steadfastly refuse to convert, even on my philosophic deathbed).

Once again, a significant source of much philosophic, mutual, and fraternal opprobrium has been revealed. So, too, in passing, I believe that I have unearthed a partial explanation for the remarkable and strange fact that philosophy has "lost touch" with the public; since the death of Dewey, not a single philosopher has attracted attention (except for the accidental notoriety enjoyed, or suffered, by Marcuse and Angela Davis) beyond the confines of the professional journals, house organs, and philosophical magazines. That is not really part of my complaint here, but an unavoidable offshoot of previous deliberations.

By this time the same doubt as crept into the brief discussion concerning the deployment of the term "knowledge" should have made itself felt with regard to *any* attempt satisfactorily to identify somebody as a philosopher, especially today, when philosophers have, by and large, given up hope of becoming "spectators of time and eternity." (This does not mean that their pomposity has vanished, however). And this leads me to my final and, I believe, most devastating reproach against those who would narrow the bounds of philosophy (or metaphilosophy) to argument (or assertion). For, what happens to our past if we decide to restrict philosophy in this manner?

For one thing, a great many individuals whom we heretofore thought of as philosophers can no longer be regarded as such. This does not bother a historian of philosophy (engaged in precisely that task, by the way) such as Flew, for he is fully prepared to exclude certain "poets" and "mystics," or, in an equally embarrassing exhibition of Western parochialism, somebody like Confucius. But what about St. Augustine? or Pascal? or Lucretius? or, on some occasions at least, Wittgenstein? And then Bergson? And last, what about a Heraclitus, one of whose *major* philosophic points is that no thesis can or should be "discussed"; it must, as the British intuitionists would likewise have it, be discerned or "seen" with the mind's eye; for he who can take the hints supplied in the Heraclitean cryptic messages is both fortunate and mentally well endowed, while he who cannot is either blind, or a victim of his own mental torpor, or both. Consequently, a Heraclitus suits his "style"—the terse, ambiguous aphorism or palindrome—to the particular appraisal of human nature, and what can (and cannot) be done about it, that he has antecedently fastened upon as his own. To ask a Heraclitus to think and write like, say, a Strawson would be to beg him to be disloyal to his own most cherished ideas. Form need not mimic content, but at least it is well advised to remain faithful to it (the same claim, as we have already witnessed, is impossible to make on behalf of those who would narrow philosophy's scope strictly to ratiocinative argumentation).

What I am suggesting is that to define philosophy as argument is to invite absurd consequences, which, if I were inclined to straitjacket the approach I am taking, would culminate in a *modus tollens* defeat of the original proposal. However, I realize that no rejection can be accomplished that quickly, and for the following reasons: first, some philosophers will not be troubled by historical counterevidence. They will uphold the Wittgensteinian dictum that "mine is the first and only world"; who cares about the past, and why should they; and if they do, why should they trouble me with it? Even Taylor, whom I regard here as on the side of the angels, is, as we saw, similarly predisposed. Second, some people who are concerned about the history of philosophy will not be bothered by the seemingly cavalier exclusion of men heretofore thought to be not only philosophers, but giants. They will reply that times change, and that conceptions of philosophy shift accordingly: we no longer consider Ptolemy a metaphysician; is that an injustice? Hume was considered a historian by his contemporaries; is it unfair that his fame is now universally agreed to lie in philosophy? We are subject to the same praise, and/or condemnation, by the ever-fluid perspectives of later generations. So why should we not at least present things as we see them, and thereby give a fairly complete picture of the mood of these times, and let history decide whether our actions have been improper, either as arrogations or as disclaimers?

Third, still others will level the charge of being an arch-irrationalist (and that's bad) at anyone who does not happen to concur with their estimate of what philosophy is. They will say that indeed, such men, insofar as they consciously profess or else inadvertently behave in accordance with some other putative norm of allegedly philosophical activity, are unworthy of being studied, let alone of being called philosophers. Generically, perhaps yes; but as exemplars of "good" philosophy, no. Such persons belong only in a museum, or a history book, or a handbook of fallacies, as illustrative lessons of what pitfalls and mistakes to avoid. They are superfluous; hence take no heed of them, except pedagogically.

Fourth and last, it will be pointed out that no one can be a philosopher without at least a rough and working definition of philosophy at his disposal, and that no definition, whether it is supposed to apply to the past or not, can possibly hope to embrace all the possible varieties of philosophic (or quasi-philosophic) reflection evenhandedly. Something will always wind up on the short end: for example, a classic definition of philosophy as the search for logically necessary propositions leaves both Hume and the late Wittgenstein out, since neither of them believes that any such propositions actually exist, not even in a diluted or technical sense of the term "exist." So we must be courageous, for the price of a global definition is superficiality and hence vacuity. Besides, no philosopher can interpret the history of the subject successfully unless his is also a philosophic focus; for him simultaneously to claim an Olympian impartiality would be disingenuous. So better by far to have convictions, and place them on the table at the outset, than to smuggle them in surreptitiously under the fictitious guise of objective reporting about philosophic predecessors. The latter approach has graver shortcomings.

If I have been over-zealous in anticipating my adversaries, and in supplying a succession of *bon mots* for them to use against me, it is not merely an act of unparalleled generosity on my part, of doing for them what they have thus far been unable, or at least unwilling, to thrash out among themselves. Nor is it symptomatic of a perverse desire to show that their thesis, that "essentially" philosophy is the instrument of argument (as Flew puts it), is after all in the right, and that I am in the end decidedly incorrect. My goal is to "prove" a slightly weaker, conditional thesis of my own: namely, that if philosophy *is* argument, then it is really not "argument" in the sense of method or technique, but in the far broader context of *general theory of justification*, and that such justification is always and ultimately about the way of life or choice between alternative courses of conduct as selected by the inquiring agent, including the decision to inquire, itself. Hence, (a) one of the logically prior things that must always be "argued" about is whether this (foregoing) position is true or not; if so, in what sense (descriptive or normative), and to what extent?; and (b) "arguments" *about*, as well as *within*, philosophy, must be ongoing, and are never to be terminated,[13] at the risk not so much of consistency as of worthwhileness and sincerity in one's commitment. The "musts" in this context I regard as imperatives, pertaining to professional ethics, in which context I see them quite simply as duties, as morally incumbent on all, not only those practitioners who feel that philosophy is best characterized in virtue of some feature or aspect of its method or style of presentation, rather than by *what* is presented, on any given occasion of performance.

As a considered afterthought, I think we must learn to get along without the expectation that philosophy can be adequately and suitably defined once and for all. If this seems more like a plea for anarchy than for freedom of thought or on behalf of tolerance, it is only so in view of

---

13. This position amounts to a small-scale espousal of the fundamentally analogous ideal championed by J. S. Mill in *On Liberty*, chap. 2; even Ross (see n11, above) pays lip-service to this ideal, while betraying its counsels in practice.

the over-optimism and exultant confidence displayed whenever a "new" philosophy, or a restructured old one, is about to be hatched or unfolded. Anyone who thinks that I stand as an advocate of unbridled chaos in intellectual affairs should examine W. D. Hudson's excellent summary of the impact of emotivism on ethical absolutists, who, once disabused of their former views, naturally come to regard "nihilism" as the only feasible alternative.[14] It is understandable that a philosopher who has been or has become disillusioned with what he has done, or with the way in which he previously went about it, should suddenly feel that the bottom has dropped out and that, unless he can stumble upon something rock-solid in a hurry, the subject he is pursuing will be unrescuable, and the world—or at least philosophy—will have to come to a premature end. Unfortunately, such ingrained reactions do not always pass away quickly.

Some will undoubtedly opine at this point that I have gone overboard in giving gratuitous advice to people who do not stand in need of it, or that I have engaged myself in an orgy of denials. But actually, my indulgence is that I have been carrying on a conversation with my own soul, or at least with the small philosophic element thereof, which, if we trust Plato, is not exactly in the worst tradition of reasoned speculation.[15] I should now like to conclude by offering a few last connecting links between the two dogmas I have sought to clarify and, where necessary, to depart from very strongly.

C. *Final remarks.* We have seen that a sizable contingent of philosophers, throughout the centuries and continuing into the present, has claimed, or at least followed, the idea that philosophy can and does yield knowledge, even though

---

14. See W. D. Hudson, *Modern Moral Philosophy* (New York: Doubleday Anchor, 1970), pp. 132-34.
15. *Theaetetus* 189E; *Sophist* 263E.

"knowledge" itself has never been pinpointed with a sufficient degree of rigor. That the knowledge supposedly derived from philosophic principles is of a special sort, allowing the knower (even if tacitly) to possess special insights
into the mysteries of life, thought, and nature, and giving
him (and his subject) a unique status, is a frequently found
corollary, more familiar to some than the more general conception with which I have taken issue, but only in rare
cases an intrinsic part of either the basic claim or the overall profession. That something to be called philosophic
knowledge, *sui generis*, is attainable indeed lingers on as an
idea, as demonstrated emphatically by the existence today of
books and courses titled "introductory" (as opposed to "in-
termediate" or even "advanced") philosophy, as though
philosophy were a subject like physics or mathematics, one
that is cumulative in its stages, and progressing from fundamental to pioneering research, as well as from easily
grasped to progressively more difficult. (In my own view,
the only tenable distinction between "introductory" and
later phases of philosophic study is one that manifests more,
and more profound, acquaintance with authors, progressive
experience with positions taken, and above all, skill in dealing with problems and categories, but this is no more "in-
termediate" or "advanced" by itself than would be, say, the
reading of 500 novels, *vs.* 250, *vs.* 125. But then the rubrics
employed are clearly intended to be more incisive, more
meaningful than just that).

We have also noticed that a number of philosophers at
present hold that philosophy *means* argument. I do not believe that this view has been made explicit or has appeared
in the literature until very recent times, yet, paradoxically,
the treatment it receives currently is most Heraclitean: it is
a proposal whose validity is taken to be self-evident, and in
need of no further elaboration or defense!

I do not hesitate to identify proponents of this second

view with contemporary adherents of the first, although I am far from suggesting, conversely, that anyone who holds the first dogma is bound to, or is committed to opt for, the second one. The reason why I am prepared to associate the protagonists of dogma 2 with the champions of dogma 1 is that for such philosophers, the step to be filled in between (2) and (1) is but a trivial and truly "self-evident" logical consequence. Anyone who maintains that philosophy is another name for argument (unless by "argument" is meant what occurs in localities and neighborhoods on hot summer nights), is going to be equally dedicated to maintaining that arguments generate, deductively or otherwise, conclusions on the basis of a group of readily assented-to and employed rules, such as logical rules of inference, or similar guidelines. The conclusions derived thus have the same status as theorems in algebra, in geometry, or for that matter in metalogic. Meanwhile, the definition of philosophy as argument is supposedly as unchallengeable as, say, an axiom, if my parallel may be extended. In short, argument yields knowledge. But philosophy and argument are equivalent, are identical. Hence, philosophy does produce knowledge, after all. It's as simple as it looks—to those who swear by it.

Unfortunately, our own history has been a merciless judge, although one not always heeded by philosophers, even when, as with Kant,[16] the verdict has come from among their own coterie. For these reasons I have deemed it high time to take on these two dogmas, the one still fashionable, the other just becoming so in our time. Philosophy still does not have anything (on these stringent terms) to show for itself, for 2,500 years of (sometimes astounding) effort. It appears to me that philosophers do themselves a disservice when insisting that knowledge is or will be forth-

16. *Critique of Pure Reason* esp. A591/B619, and A630/B658; also, B xxx.

coming shortly—just be patient, they counsel themselves and the outside world, which, as Kant sharply noted, has already long been fed up with philosophy altogether.[17] Not only do we encourage false optimism, but, by insisting that the worst is over instead of yet to come, we distort the subject, or, as Austin aptly observed, what remains of it, and so make it even less likely that we shall ever find out just *what* philosophers have actually been doing all these years. Maybe we are too sensitive, too afraid of being embarrassed, but in the process of hiding this we are embarrassing ourselves, without ever realizing it. Perhaps "justification" of what we are up to, to reassure ourselves that we are not quacks, charlatans, or parasites, is another idol, a false god, a crutch that we really should dispose of, and quickly. Maybe Wittgenstein's remark: "What does mathematics need a foundation for?"[18] is equally pertinent to philosophy's own miserable condition. Perhaps the "good angel's" continued blessing and favor are all that we really require.

When I am asked "What is your philosophy?" I should like one day to be sufficiently emboldened to confess in Socratic reply: "I don't know; and neither does anyone else. I should really like to find out, even if the experience proves hard to bear or undergo; but I cannot as yet dare, because two dogmas of philosophy stand in my way, so that I cannot accept the manure in front of my path for what it is." Until now I have not had the spirit even to think such "dangerous (and untimely) thoughts." But who knows, the philosophic winds may yet change their direction.

17. *Prolegomena*, Appendix ("The world is tired of metaphysical assertions. . .").
18. L. Wittgenstein, *Remarks on the Foundations of Mathematics*, trans. G. E. M. Anscombe (Cambridge, Mass.: MIT Press, 1956), Part V, 13, p. 171. *Cf. Zettel*, trans. G. E. M. Anscombe (Berkeley and Los Angeles: University of California Press, 1970), no. 301 p. 55e ("He must go on like this *without a reason*"), and no. 315 p. 58e (" 'Why do you demand explanations? . . .' ").

2
Understanding Philosophy

magine if you will a trained archaeologist say, 5,000 years from now, attempting to dig up the remains of what we call our contemporary civilization, and to make some sense of them in the light of his own, as well as through developments that have occupied the intervening five millennia. Now suppose such a person were to come across only one item, but one that surely did play a significant role in the culture of the late twentieth century: an empty Coke bottle. Let us hypothesize for a moment that the archaeologist is faced with the task of reconstructing our entire civilization on the basis of that, and that alone. What will he say? What would we say, in his place?

Doubtless the first thing anyone would do would be to examine the bottle very carefully. Apart from the name and the trademark, which might permit much philological speculation, what is there to comment upon? Only the curious statement to be found (we hope) somewhere on the bottom, reading "No deposit, no return." No deposit, no return. What do we make of it, putting ourselves in the archaeologist's position?

Let us think for a minute. Suppose we know nothing at all about a culture, and wish to learn something. Suppose, further, that the materials at our disposal are scant. Anything we venture to affirm will be inherently risky, but at the same time, no one is in a position to disprove our contentions, whatever they might be. What is it that we should *most* like to know about this strange, bygone civilization, since it intrigues us so much and inasmuch as we are not likely to be able to piece together very much of what went on; what is it that fascinates us, and attracts (and holds) our attention? In a word, the *beliefs* that animated the peoples of that time, again in the light of whatever advances in human knowledge may have been made subsequently. To paraphrase Comte's three stages of history, we should like to know something about their superstitions, their religions, and their science, such as they each were, remaining aware that the categories we choose may not exactly apply, or may collapse into one another, when we come to discover the belief-structure into which we are inquiring.

In this spirit, consider that enigmatic proposition "No deposit, no return" for a second time. With a little imagination, the following case can be made: "deposit" in all likelihood refers to some tribute to the gods, whoever they were, of that epoch. Similarly, the word "return" must refer to an afterlife, or a return to one's mortal status: a kind of metempsychosis. The insertion of the negative term ("no") means that "No deposit, no return" issues a warning, perhaps a threat of some kind. Although there is only one Coca-Cola bottle left on this earth, let us say that we possess enough evidence to support the conclusion that at one time there were hundreds of thousands, perhaps millions, of these bottles in use, strewn all over the world. So our tireless efforts to unravel the mysteries surrounding this long-buried civilization have, as it seems, been justly rewarded. We have now "discovered" something about their moral code and their religion simultaneously. Even better, we have "found" something whose human role during this well-nigh prehistoric period was universal, not subject to limitations of language, geography, race, or other discriminating factors. We may even infer that the tribute in question was that of drinking the liquid inside the bottle, as a guarantee that the individual who did so either would become, or at least assure himself of remaining, immortal. Whether Coke was itself a god, or merely a missionary from the gods, is unclear; but we can tell from the shape of the bottle that not just gods, but goddesses as well, were involved in the religious ritual of Coke-drinking whose specific details are lost to us, along with the rubble of what conceivably were once pagan temples erected to honor both the divine elixir and the heavenly form outlined on the vessel that contained it. Such treasures await the man who may yet, armed with shovel and spade, uncover what little is left on the face of the earth from that long-distant era, only to confirm our hypothesis!

A clever philologist might also be able to defend such a theory from the attacks that it would surely undergo at the hands of scholars writing for the professional journals of later times. They might object that *no* here is a compressed way of saying "it is unnecessary to" and consequently that the entire meaning of the oracular pronouncement on the bottom of each and every (we surmise) Coke bottle is to be regarded in a changed light. The language-scholar might retort that *no* is to be construed on the model of one of the few extant pieces of writing from that time, a precious numbered scrap of paper bearing the equally baffling slogan "no tickee, no shirtee." (Since the context makes it impossible to deduce that this is, or was, a laundry stub, it carries equal weight in the eyes of the principal investigators. But even if they knew what it was, or was used for, a laundry stub and a Coke bottle would remain on a par; so the sheerly linguistic point is unaffected). Here the controversy rests, awaiting the enlightenment of future toilers laboring in the vineyards of research.

Before this charmingly implausible account grows tedious, let us retreat from it and draw some appropriate morals. In no way is this story intended to ridicule either religion or scholarship, although such a satire may be among its by-products. Rather, the main point concerns what might pompously be entitled "methodology in the interpretation of the history of philosophy," and the bearing of this on the pursuit called philosophizing. I have chosen to call this "understanding philosophy," because I believe that understanding the history of philosophy is integral to the philosophic enterprise. By the term "history of philosophy" I include movements as well as authors, "isms" as well as texts; patterns of ideas, as well as *ipsissima verba*, and, in addition, the methodology of the history of philosophy, more simply called historiography. It should be borne in mind that by "understanding philosophy" I have my own understanding in mind, and neither claim nor pretend to speak for anyone else.

The anecdote just recounted is meant to illustrate, in a painless way, the types of problems that beset historicophilosophical scholarship in certain areas. For example, the field of pre-Socratic philosophy is one in which we possess (up to Parmenides) little or nothing in the way of a continuous narrative, be it dialogue or lecture; indeed,

Heraclitus, inaugurating a trend to be followed by such diverse figures as Pascal and Nietzsche, respectively, actually prefers to state his ideas aphoristically, and so they have come down to us, as though they were the stylistic forerunners of Nietzsche and Wittgenstein. But Heraclitus's predecessors did not write in riddles or epigrams; the impression that they so conveyed their thoughts is the result of tragic accidents occuring in the checkered history of the transmission of their works. This is well known; what is not so well established, or accepted, is the thesis that since we do not have much to go on, we might as well do the best possible job with what we do have on hand. And "best" in this context means that we ought to try to extract the maximum possible insight from the fragments that have been preserved, both singly and collectively; we should do whatever we can to enrich their meaning and to make their conceptions as profound as we can. There will naturally be disagreements as to what is deep and what shallow; but since these turn up with depressing familiarity wherever we turn in philosophy, we should not be afraid to let them appear here as well.

The recommendation just adopted is not likely to win the approval of numerous "orthodox" historians of classical philosophy. These scholars would insist on sticking to the text. But what text? There is none; only sentences, sandwiched by eternal silence. Quite responsibly, they urge a cool appraisal of the evidence. What evidence? The testimony of Plato and Aristotle, not to mention various Alexandrian writers of more or less doubtful reliability in many instances. And even Plato and Aristotle are hardly unimpeachable sources, as a notable succession of writers from H. F. Cherniss[1] onward has made abundantly clear. Fidel-

1. H. F. Cherniss, *Aristotle's Criticism of PreSocratic Philosophy* (Baltimore: Johns Hopkins Press, 1935), and *Aristotle's Criticism of Plato and the Academy* (Baltimore: Johns Hopkins Press, 1944).

163719

ity to text and to historical fact is quite noble, although by
no means the sole ideal to be followed; but does it apply
here? The trained archaeologist, faced with the temptations
engendered by the Coke remonstration, might recoil from
drawing the conclusions that a rasher scientist would wish
to espouse. How is one to adjudicate between authorities,
where little or nothing is known, and still less is likely ever
to be added to the store of information within one's reach?
In such circumstances, the traditional rules of scholarship,
or of impartial investigation, are sheerly irrelevant, pending
further developments. This does *not* mean that they should
be laid aside altogether, or that they are valueless for di-
recting research into areas where, thankfully, our supply of
materials and facts is less slender. Nor does it mean that it
is not worthwhile to codify and systematize some rules, and
to evaluate, from a methodological perspective, the performance of historical inquirers themselves, making allowances
for the undeniable fact that tastes and fashions in methodology will change as readily as will anything else.

What it does mean is that on certain occasions the scholarly rules, whatever they are, become inapplicable and
therefore should be suspended. Instead, another criterion
should be put forward: that of "illumination." Does the interpretation offered, say, of an Anaximander, shed light on
something philosophical (e.g., the nature of injustice and
strife, or the metaphysical theory of growth and decay, or
change through time), or does it not? Does it improve our
understanding of the subject, and if so, how? Admittedly,
the criterion seems vague, because its formulation will differ from scholar to scholar. What sounds illuminating to
Jaspers will not please Heidegger; and what Heidegger
thinks sheds light on some topic will seem unintelligible
and, moreover, a willful distortion to Cassirer. But this is
only symptomatic of the general malaise in philosophy,
stemming from the fact that it lacks a recognized

"decision-procedure" for resolution of its disputes; and, as has already been said, we should not shrink from such controversy merely because it is so unpleasant a spectacle; after all, controversy pervades philosophy at every level, and obtains in the implicit contrast between almost any two (or more) thinkers.

I am definitely *not* saying, however, that there is no room for different kinds of methods in historiography; only, that the limitations of each type display themselves at various turns. No one would think of a doxographical report as embodying the whole of what wisdom there is to be gained from philosophy and the study of its career; but it has its usefulness, at the beginning of an education, and as a supplement thereafter. Historical methods, unlike philosophies they describe, are not (generally) incompatible, or mutually exclusive, although they may well compete for the favor of scholars. They have, instead, their areas of applicability, whose boundaries are as ill-defined and as flexible as the different branches of philosophy that they fain would treat (consider whether the free-will question belongs in ethics, in metaphysics, or in both).

What this shows is that there is no acceptable way for the student of comparative methodology to satisfy everyone, short of inventing a comprehensive philosophy of his own, one from which may be deduced certain principles encompassing (among other things) historiography. But to do this is equally to incur the contempt of some future scholars who will detect a bias in all judgments rendered about philosophy's past and its individual representatives, while also courting the wrath of those philosophic peers, past, present and future, who do or would still disagree on more ultimate points. The most nagging question remains: if it is unsatisfactory to view the story of philosophy through, say, Aristotelian or Hegelian lenses, is it equally improper to view them through anybody else's, precisely because they are not one's own? And if they *are* one's own (e.g. if one is Aristotle or Hegel) is the same charge vindicated, on the slightly different grounds that the specific theories propounded are, to be blunt, false, because their logico-metaphysical understructure is obsolete, inadequate, or defective?

If philosophy is "dead," then it stands to reason that the history of philosophy is the whole of philosophy. If philosophy is "alive," however, then the history of philosophy is in jeopardy, and may be crowded out. The history of science belongs, not to science, but to history, while science is an ongoing, "progressive" enterprise. If philosophy were in this fortunate position (at least, some would call it fortunate), it would have no need, and even less use, for its history. This would become a mere curiosity, to be relegated to the sphere of humanistic learning and erudition. Mathematicians interest themselves in logarithms, not in Napier; in Pappus's theorem, not in Pappus's biography. But, if no philosophy is or can be absolutely true; if extant as well as conceivable "systems" are alike doomed to failure; and if, in knowing that, and why, philosophic theories do not and cannot achieve ultimate vindication when placed under objective scrutiny, we somehow are unable to become much wiser in the process, or to gain philosophic understanding from bouts with disappointment, then it is time for someone to write philosophy's obituary, and for this task the history of philosophy seems preeminently suited. Hegel's Owl of Minerva remark, made in the historical context of observing how philosophy arose while a civilization around it was deteriorating, becomes appropriate here in a narrower vein. Similarly, while the fortunes of a given philosophy are declining, or so the argument goes, the history of that philosophy must be thriving, because there is, it seems, nothing left to do but record the adventures of something that has, for good or ill, become passé, if not a landmark falsehood.

It is therefore easy to see why so much hostility and tension prevail between historians of philosophy and so-called creative philosophers (not that this is always the case). The logician or phenomenologist who is passionate about some dogma, slogan, or method is understandably impatient with those who wish to incorporate in their frequently plodding and sometimes eclectic way the partial but valuable insights of the past; while the competent historian, usually a person wedded to some form of "naturalism" if not historicism, is one who has seen ideas come and ideas go, is weary of the whole procession, and is mistrustful, indeed downright skeptical, of the impetuous claims of some of his less erudite colleagues. He is, moreover, often convinced that there is indeed nothing new under the sun, nothing more left to say. He is therefore prone to take a paternalistic attitude toward the past, and perhaps even to point to the alleged wisdom to be derived from a careful study of, for example, The Great Books which in the view of the constructive philosopher of the present (at any given time) may seem dead in the sense of having nothing further to contribute, nothing that has not already been developed, or else is entailed, by the system, theory, or method of which he is a devoted partisan. Meanwhile, the philosophic "commitments" of the historian are usually sufficiently bland to be universally acceptable without, as James would say, making a difference at all; and these inanities at least function in a way that permits the historian to claim a dual role as a philosopher, still emphasizing his congenial neturality and impartiality as an investigator into philosophy's course of development; only the historian never really manages to remain in reasonably good standing at all times with parties from both "camps."

Let us return to the archaeologist and the Coke bottle. Here is a prime example of someone's getting "too much" out of a reconstruction of the past. But it is only "too much" because we know it to be so. In 5,000 years from now, it may seem a very judicious comment on our way of life. There is no guarantee that we know ourselves better than others will someday be able to; for while we enjoy, to use Ryle's *mot*, "privileged access" into the tempo of contemporary existence, we may lack the detachment with which to differentiate between the trivial and the sublime, the profound and the meaningless. This is especially likely in an age so inundated, so bombarded with ideas and thoughts and "messages" and "communications" as ours is, with little or no time to sit back and contemplate life, and perhaps no accurate way to look at ourselves, except by looking at those whom we are following. The same frustrating variation on the theme of incessant reflection about ourselves during the era of our own lives may remain valid for the future, enabling generations after us to come to grips with us, but not, alas, with themselves. The tragedy of the quest for self-knowledge is that it is, perhaps necessarily, incomplete—a task that perpetually awaits completion, but is fulfilled, if at all, only after our departure from the scene.

In this context, I venture to say that the archaeologist's immediate inspiration may not be misplaced, after all. Who are we to judge that his interpretation is a mistake? Perhaps, fanciful though it be, it tells us more about ourselves, albeit indirectly, than we are willing to admit. But even if it is entirely wrong, it is at least *interesting;* and I suggest that, in certain life atmospheres and intellectual endeavors, interest should replace plain truth-or-falsity as the standard by which to measure a worthwhile effort. Though the construal of "No deposit, no return" be ever so mistaken, it answers to an entirely different—not necessarily higher, but not lower, either—standard from mere accuracy or inaccuracy. Again, this does not imply that the "plain, historical method" (in Locke's case, it was plain psychological) is worthless, only that it is not canonic, and neither is any substitute for it, including any of one's own novel proposals.

Of course, "interest" is a subjective standard; but, to repeat a tiresome line, so are most philosophic canons. That
is no reason to abandon them, unless one is prepared to re-
nounce philosophy in its entirety (whatever that may mean)
along with it. The main point is not to counsel tolerance of
divergent points of view, although that is certainly one of
the subsidiary objectives. Nor is it merely to encourage
scholars to "get something more out of" what they are
doing than slavish adherence to prevailing norms of doxographical, historical method would allow, although that, too,
is to be fostered. Rather, the attempt being made is to raise
and confront two related issues: doctrinal attribution, and
the evidential status of available primary sources; and how
together they bear on the tasks facing every philosopher.

If one were to accuse the archaeologist of falsifying the
data upon which he is exercising his talents, he could at
least reply that in the absence of qualifications, his guess
was as valid as anyone else's. He might also add, and this is
crucial, that while the originator of "No deposit, no return"
(or perhaps it was a joint product, requiring as many cola
theologians as there once were Homers) may not ever have
intended something "religious" by that starkly dramatic,
chiseled inscription, this is an internally consistent, coherent, and significant way of looking at the aphorism.
Moreover, the archaeologist is aware that *without* the
enigmatic legend on the Coke bottle, he would never have
been suitably inspired to come up with his interpretation,
questionable though it may seem. In this sense, the saying,
in all its pithiness, is very much the source for the archaeologist's reconstruction; of that there cannot be any
doubt. Restated, the existence of the Coca-Cola admonition
is a necessary condition for the production of the (or any)
worthwhile interpretation placed upon it; it cannot be
fashioned otherwise, unless to credit the archaeologist with
undeserved originality.

Similarly, when Aristotle disarmingly "credits" Plato with

having foreshadowed the introduction of the concept of final causality, when Hegel sees more than the rest of us can in promoting the reconciliation of theoretical differences obtaining between and among philosophers, when Jaspers reads his own "ciphers of transcendence" willy-nilly into Nietzsche and Kant, when Heidegger claims that Parmenides adumbrates the heralded "ontological difference" and in so doing "anticipates" the teachings of Heidegger's own philosophy; what is going on? Is it merely another instance of arrogant presumption on the part of the philosopher, that everybody thinks (or should, if he has anything meaningful to say) like himself? This is certainly what Cherniss makes of Aristotle—but Cherniss is an avowed Platonist! Is it perhaps an attempt to convert readers to one's own philosophy, as James tried to do in reciting the long and fictitious "history of pragmatism" stemming from Socrates and culminating in J. S. Mill? Is it a usurpation of previous doctrines and tenets, bent maliciously to suit later purposes? The answers will depend in part on whether one thinks the philosopher in question was honest or lacked integrity. Since this is a biographical matter, and not easy to investigate from the texts themselves, philosophy is then threatened with the Nietzschean possibility of being turned into admiration of the exceptional personality. This is not surprising; it formed as well as plagued the living experience of the Academy and the Lyceum during their most glorious years. Moreover, the disposition of a philosopher is often an ineradicable element in his philosophy—Socrates, Plotinus, and Spinoza are unquestionably the most noteworthy examples, and St. Augustine is not far behind them. So these questions cannot be peremptorily dismissed as *ad hominem* puerilities. Nevertheless, they are not susceptible to any general technique of analysis: reactions will vary, as we consult philosopher after philosopher, in their sometime capacity as

historians of their own field. What, then, can we say that
could be regarded as a set of individual yet uniformly
binding recommendations?

Only this:

1. Every philosopher is attempting to *unify his own experience*[2] (this insight appears to have been first noted, although not originally practiced, by Ralph Waldo Emerson).
Some achieve it through a metaphysical doctrine, others
through a "self-integrating power" (e.g., God), while some
remain diffident about the possibility of achieving this,
while trying to do so nonetheless (e.g., Hume).

2. In attempting to unify his own experience, any
philosopher who attempts to convey his "voyage of discovery" to others and in so doing, to share both the journey
and its destination with them, will adopt a language and
format he considers suitable for that purpose. (This may
help to account for bizarre differences in style and terminology that pervade philosophy, notwithstanding repeated efforts to find a common vocabulary, such as were
made by Aristotle and Wolff, or to promote an agreed-upon
technique of reasoning, such as was championed by Leibniz).

3. Philosophers quite naturally appropriate the categories
and/or dimensions through which they perceive and order
what they may care to designate as "reality," to do yeoman
service in other areas—including historiography. This explains why a philosopher will fervently "locate" a particular
doctrine in one of his intellectual forebears, when to the
naive or the uncommitted reader it does not appear to be
there. The philosopher takes the liberty of "imposing" his

2. Or, as Søren Kierkegaard writes, to achieve "the unification of the successive
in the simultaneous," i.e., the organization of personal commitments across both
permanent and momentary or episodic spans of time, which is the defining
medium of conscious human existence. *Concluding Unscientific Postscript*, trans.
D. F. Swenson and W. Lowrie (Princeton, N.J.: Princeton University Press,
1941), pp. 311, 365, 371.

categories on someone else's ideas, inasmuch as he believes in the soundness of his own present point of view— regardless of whether he will continue to do so in the future, whether his conception of reality is one that allows for change—or denies change in favor of positing some allegedly immutable, incorruptible entity (through axioms of value or in descriptive propositions). To accuse the philosopher of bias, or of obtrusive axe-grinding, is tacitly to assert that his way of looking at the world leaves something to be desired, or is faulty (for if it were not, how could one object to it?). The historian who takes this *modus tollens* line of refutation spares himself the work of examining the particular philosophy; he merely rules it out in advance as an alleged misapplication, or overextension, into the area of his special expertise. (And so we are thrown back to the tiresome conflict waged between some historians and many philosophers).

4. The presumption must always be in favor of a philosopher's moral integrity, if there is no solid evidence to the contrary (as there is with Francis Bacon and with Leibniz, for example; but even there the issue of integrity is clouded by deep factual disputes over the misrepresentation of the conditions that would-be detractors describe as pertaining to their respective lives and careers). If a philosopher goes so far as to mention a predecessor approvingly, then, although the basis for his approval may be poorly reasoned or even nonexistent, there is every reason to believe that the philosopher paying the compliment is sincere, else why would he even bother to mention a competitor or potential rival? This does not entail that a disparaging reference automatically is a charge of dishonesty, nor that it operates to the disadvantage of the accuser; for on the contrary, one generally discusses "mistaken" views only when one is compelled to take them sufficiently seriously, or else to hold them in esteem and honor. This is

why I maintain that the *presumption* should be unwaveringly in favor of a philosopher's own uprightness at least in matters concerning the articulation and rejection or defense of ideas, his own as well as others'.

Consequently, when philosopher X tells us that he finds something valuable (though it or X may be in error in certain respects) in the thought of philosopher Y, even if X's interpretation is not the last word on the subject, neither is Y's, or anyone else's, for that matter. What then is the last "authority" for the "correct" reading of a philosopher? The authoritative, but unparadoxical, reply is that there is none. This does not mean that there are no experts who do qualify in a secondary sense as genuine authorities; but there is no authori*ty*, anymore than there is *the* philosopher—the understandable and legitimately motivated admiration for Aristotle by Thomas Aquinas notwithstanding. In philosophy there are no authorities, as Friedrich Waismann once (unauthoritatively) observed—and, if one wishes the support of a distinguished parallel, one need only consider the sciences. At least there are no *human* authorities, although there are true experts aplenty. But science, like philosophy, is the deliberate product of human beings; it does not exist in a separate realm, detached from its creators (although its results are validated on an intersubjective basis). From this quasi-reductive argument, it follows that, since there are no human authorities, there is no authority of any kind to be appealed to, period. We just have to learn to live with less. And philosophy is not unique in this respect—witness art; look at science.

However, the main, recurring point has yet to be touched on anew. If X claims to discover something from his reading of Y, this is X's way of telling us that without Y, X would not have been led to the insight he arrived at. In this sense, the relationship between philosopher and reader, or between two entrenched philosophers who confront each other through the written or spoken word, is ideally that of *stimulus* and *response*, what Heidegger calls "a timeless dialogue between thinkers," one that is "governed by other rules" than those which apply between a historian and a philosopher of the past. (Consequently the drift of the respective interpretations offered will differ as well, which is not to imply that they *necessarily* conflict with, rather than complement, each other). This judgment is partially vindicated even in those cases where a doctrine held by X appears arbitrarily fastened around Y's neck. For the philosopher can always aver (and Heidegger, for one, does) that it was reading Y that initially prompted him to think up the tenet that he then proceeded to expound at first without reference to Y, only to "ground" it in Y's text upon a fresh or a subsequent rereading. In many cases then, X is *crediting* Y with being the necessary catalytic agent or condition (and sometimes the sufficient condition) supplying the intellectual climate in which X's thought was born and able to emerge and flourish. To this extent, X is disclaiming personal originality as well, instead admitting that his views are at least partially derivative from ideas extant in one or more of his predecessors, or perhaps merely a novel synthesis or combination, as, for example, Hegel sometimes claimed on behalf of his own system. This is never an easy acknowledgment for any serious thinker to make, but when it is made, it should be seen as a serious and respectful tribute, although not necessarily taken literally (this applies to the excessive modesty of St. Thomas, in *re* Aristotle, for example).

When it is said that some idea is "Platonic," to cite just one tradition, it does not mean, and it does not *have* to mean, that it corresponds precisely to something discerned from the enigmatic texts and ultimately unfathomable authorial intentions of Plato himself. It may mean adherence to some ideology or world view whose strains previously have been identified, in virtue of certain prominent features or characteristics (otherworldliness, faith in mathematics as a model of or a method for reaching metaphysical truth, reliance on myth to create reverence for and to illustrate the conception of moral virtue, belief in the existence of an abstraction called "the Good," or in human preexistence as purely knowing beings, etc.). But there is room for another usage, according to which "Platonic" could suggest "it may not be in Plato or in one of his followers, but it is inspired by reading Plato and would not have been thought of, much less developed, without him." That is far too cumbersome an expression, however, and so it is proper to content ourselves with the use of the misleadingly curt epithet "Platonic," which, therefore, occasionally requires a protracted and pedantic explanation such as this.

The repetition of instances in the history of philosophy wherein someone, perhaps incorrectly but always out of genuine respect, credits a predecessor with an accomplishment, is an eloquent testimony to the fact that philosophy cannot—not merely refuses to, but is in no position to—do without its past. Of course, this argument will not hold for someone who proclaims that "mine is the first and only world," whether this indicates a defense of solipsism or merely the presence of an ahistorical attitude. Nor is the history of philosophy the kind of sound but embarrassing evidence one wants to admit, when it is precisely the status of that discipline and its contents that are at stake, when numberless philosophers may be equally prepared at every moment to set up their own philosophy, or that which they have borrowed from others, as the Ultimate Arbiter, the standard, not so much by which other things are judged (see point 3, above), but by which all else is made to look antiquated. The only effective counterattack is to cite again what history reveals: repeated confident assertions, followed by frustration and evident failure. So while the historians sometimes are tempted to maintain that philosophy has no future (else how could one write intelligibly about it while it is still "in process"?) the antihistorical, overconfident philosophers for their part are not prepared to learn from history, but are ready to rush headlong into a virtually unavoidable repetition of the same old blunders, errors that fuel the historian's professional skepticism and intellectual agnosticism once more.

This brings us back to a further, reinforcing point, that texts (primary sources), while valuable, do not constitute the Last Word, either. This belief is held for at least two reasons: (1) if we were limited to extracting from texts the lessons ostensibly taught by the great philosophers as well as the minor ones, we should never learn anything, since the "correct" interpretation of not a single one of these men is or is ever likely to be definitively established or settled. And perhaps there is some consolation in this state of affairs, since it permits us to gain a far richer variety of interpretations, and renewed encounters with both the masters and their intellectual underlings, than would otherwise be possible. (2) Moreover, if, for example, The Great Books were our sole source of wisdom, we should be hopelessly handicapped in studying periods for which there are no books or records left at all; methodologically, we would be debarred even from attempting to study the pre-Socratics; somehow, we cannot escape feeling that we would then be worse off, instead of blessed in our ignorance of "how it actually was." In short, reliance on *ipsissima verba* is fine, but when it becomes an obsession, it blocks, in the stirringly foreboding words of C. S. Peirce, the road to inquiry; and that is plainly undesirable, although we may never be in a position to perceive, much less care, that the road to inquiry is sometimes blocked because of our own folly and narrow-mindedness.

This is not yet complete. The study of the history of ideas shows us that movements and "isms" are *not* merely the sum total of the dispersion of the effects of primary and secondary sources. Vico's *New Science* (1725) was not read before Michelet, nor outside Italy, and yet it was, miraculously, "understood," in large part, through the flight of rumor during the first century after its publication. We shall probably never understand quite how this happened, but it did. Somebody *had* to have read it, and yet nobody *did!* The facts are there, but the picture they present is comically unintelligible. Locke's *Essay* and *Two Treatises*, on the other hand, were widely read almost from the beginning, and yet, in spite of their eventual fame, their tenets were not being received or entertained seriously, let alone winning general acceptance, until from their dates of publication some twenty years had passed, by which time Locke was safely in his grave.[3] The history of philosophy needs, therefore, to be accompanied by a regular study of *patterns* of influence, which serves as a corrective in its own right to the convenient, but historically wrong, notion that primary sources are both philosophically *and* philhistorically canonic. In fact, they are neither, although this does not deny their intrinsic value one whit; indeed, it is enhanced thereby.

What philosophy is desperately in search of in this or at any time, is a developed theory of *analogy*. Not the Platonic, nor the Thomistic kind, but one that is consciously reflective and linguistically self-referential: that is, one that might help to illuminate for us just what philosophy is *like*. All comparisons are double-edged and therefore dangerous, but the risk, if taken prudently, is

3. Roughly the same thing is true, with appropriate modifications, of the early fate of Kant's critical masterpieces.

usually well worth the exposure. In my opinion, until such time as an adequate, comprehensive, and definitive theory of what philosophy is, or is like, can hope to make an appearance, whether under the guise of "metaphilosophy" or as the fruit of of "normal" philosophical research, we shall continue to be justified in challenging the prevailing and often lackluster norms of scholarship; in contenting ourselves by simply examining bits and pieces of the landscape, and providing interpretations of the scenes portrayed, which might frequently be representations that are beyond the wildest dreams of their originators. Once we *know* what philosophy comprises, then and only then shall we be in a strong position to wield that axe, and to separate in an unbiased way the properly philosophical from the "extraneous," purely historical material. Since philosophers have repeatedly tried, and just as frequently failed, to supply such a theory, and to answer the question "what is Philosophy (like)?" there can be no legitimate ban on methods of textual criticism as outrageous or inapplicable, at least not in advance of their concrete employment. Apriorism in what in some quarters is called hermeneutics is as out of place in philosophy as it is elsewhere, for an indefinite period yet to come, I feel. At least, such is the formidable challenge I issue.

To understand philosophy means to realize that philosophers have been engaged in a constant, self-defeating, and heretofore unsatisfactory struggle for vindication of their own occupation as a reliable form of knowledge-yielding inquiry. To become aware of this is to promote a certain freedom in one's own approach to the delineation of this apparently vain, yet ceaseless and fascinating battle. Our future archaeologist examining the Coke bottle therefore has every reason to rejoice, and as philosophers we have no right to ridicule or laugh at him, only at ourselves. In fact, insofar as we discuss and criticize the culture and the philosophers of the past, we might do well to emulate, not replace, his methods. Perhaps we, too, shall discover something in ourselves of which heretofore we had been oblivious. The spur to edification is well worth taking up, instead of the axe.

3

Philosophic Utterances:
An "Existential" Theory

I

1 *Introduction.* Everyone is acquainted with certain specimens of philosophic discourse: "the unexamined life is not worth living," "the real is the rational, the rational is the real," "know thyself," "I think, therefore I am," and the like. I want to present a theory of the nature of these kinds of communications in this paper. This will amount to a theory concerning the nature of philosophic inquiry, but that is unavoidable, and it would be undesirable to attempt to avoid it. I do not claim originality for the theory; its main inspiration stems from some remarks by Kierkegaard. I do not claim comprehensiveness for the theory; no doubt there are many intellectual areas to which it does scant justice, and some of these fields may qualify as philosophic. I do suggest that the theory deserves attention, not least for the philosophic vision (and the vision of philosophy) inherent in it, views which, where they are implicit, I shall do my best to iterate.

2. *Ground Rules.* At the outset it is wise to insist on making one distinction while eschewing another. I wish to undertake the exposition (and defense) of a theory of philosophic assertions. This is not the same as a philosophic theory of assertions. My concern is not with general features of semantics, nor with the relation between language and the world or "reality." Such theories have received much attention of late, as the "speech acts" movement in Anglo-American philosophy testifies. My interest lies solely in describing what might be regarded as a small but proper subset of a general theory of assertions, namely, so-called philosophic assertions. I shall not discuss the relations between the wider theory and the narrower portion thereof which I shall examine, although I shall freely appropriate certain "models" of the nature of discourse and apply them to philosophic contexts in a way that I hope will be illuminating. Nor am I going to claim that the larger theory is necessarily isomorphic with that part of it that will occasion scrutiny. The reader who wishes to extrapolate a theory of language from this paper may be sorely disappointed, but then only if any misguided expectations are retained.

The reader should also observe, however, that I am not in a hurry to make formulations neat or precise. I shall use all available vocabulary at my disposal, with no immediate effort to attain what passes for linguistic rigor. Such terms as "assertion," "utterance," "statement," "proposition," "proposal," "sentence," "thought," and the like will be used interchangeably. I see no harm in this; it draws attention to the fact that choice of terminology is, for present purposes, sheerly arbitrary, a matter of individual preference, and therefore inessential. I am not worried here whether failure to distinguish such expressions from one another leads to ambiguities of reference, still less whether in using them I am inadvertently "committing" myself to the existence (in some sense of *that* word) of abstract entities. Shocking as it may sound to some, I have far more important things to disclose, and the point of this paper is to share them with the reader.

3. *Preliminary apology*. Having said this, the reader may wonder what the advantages of my approach might be. The forthcoming theory of philosophic utterances must be able to speak on its own behalf. However, this should be added: the theory is in no way "reductive." As mentioned in the introduction, I do not claim to assimilate all branches of philosophy (let alone of its history) under a single heading. Still less is there in the theory to be preferred any room for an explanation of philosophic discourse by accounting for its origins. While there are grave contemporary doubts as to whether the "genetic fallacy" is indeed a fallacy (as opposed to the alleged fallacy committed by those who regularly invoke the genetic fallacy as an accusatory device), the reader will search in vain both for such rubrics and for such explanations of philosophic activity in this chapter. I do not suggest that there is no value in such work; the Wittgenstein-oriented "psychoanalytic theories of philosophy," which have attained some vogue in recent times, enjoy a deserved attractiveness. I only hope that the theory about to be elaborated is not without its own fascination and charm. I offer it neither as an alternative nor as a rival theory; it should stand or fall on its own merits, or intrinsically.

4. *Initial formulation.* Philosophic utterances exhibit a number of depth-characteristics (as opposed, in some instances, to their surface grammar; in other cases, compatible, or even identical therewith). The most significant of these, in my judgment, is that they are *future-tensed.* That is, they uniformly refer to some event or state of affairs that is to take place or come about at some later time than that of the assertion. It follows that in some rough sense philosophic statements are *predictions.* The question is, precisely what do they predict, and how? I maintain that they predict in a normative sense; that is, they predict that which ought to happen. They are therefore *deontological* in character.

At this point the reader has every right to suspect an inconsistency. He may well ask, how can a statement predict that something will be the case and at the same time be normative in scope? We know that what should be frequently is not, or does not turn out to be, the case. Moreover, to claim that philosophic thoughts belong to the domain of deontology is to say, in effect, that they constitute *imperatives* of some kind. An imperative would lose its point if the state of affairs that it postulates as a desiderate were already in existence, if the prospects for its realization in the natural course of events were favorable. To these criticisms I reply, for the moment, by asking the reader to suspend judgment on such matters, at least until an elaboration of the theory is complete; for then objections shall be considered anew. For a truly unprejudiced inquiry to have a chance for success, I must now abjure any guarantee that the outcome of renewal of such criticism as just outlined will not be devastating to the theory in its provisional as well as its final forms.

A philosophic statement expresses, then, an imperative of some sort, although the imperative may well be revealed rather than concealed by the grammatical form of the sentence. What class of imperatives are we dealing with? Here we must trot out a qualification. I should rather call it an *injunction* than an imperative. The difference is this: the concept of "imperative" implies something universal in extent. In the case of Kantian categorical imperatives, what is universal is the scope of application; the imperative "binds" everyone to its stated norm. Hypothetical imperatives specify the most efficient available means for reaching a given end that has been approved on reflection, among those means that are also morally commensurate with that end. They therefore prescribe a certain fitness-relation that holds regardless of time or place, just so long as the circumstances that provide the hypothetical imperative with its field of application remain the same, or effective in promoting whatever end is first taken as paradigmatic. But the kind of injunction that philosophic statements embody is *singulary* in extent; it applies to at least one person, but also affects at most one person. *It dictates a course of conduct to be followed by but one agent: namely, the philosopher propounding it.*

From this it might seem that philosophic utterances are "self-referential" or self-inclusive, but this way of putting it is misleading, inasmuch as it implies that the scope of the statement is self-predicative, *among other things.* Not so; it is self-predicative, period. Moreover, since philosophic assertions postulate a certain course of action to be pursued, I prefer to call them *self-instantiating,*[1] as one way of designating interplay between statement and whatever such statement calls for. What the statement calls for is something (or some action) beyond itself, which is why I would refuse to allow the "self-referential" interpretation to pass without comment. That philosophic "propositions" are not really propositions at all, but instead an unusual species of *command,* has by now (on my construal) been established.

1. I owe this term to R. S. Brumbaugh, who uses it throughout his *Plato for the Modern Age* (New York: Collier, 1962).

This furnishes the rationale for considering them imperatives of a unique variety. But it must be understood that the referent of the command is personal, and purely so; it binds only the agent (the philosopher) delivering the command, and is therefore *self-prescriptive* only. I trust that no more need be said on this subject, for it is not my intention to concentrate on finding the exact equivalents in semantic jargon. Our explicative tools, as the ground rules elaborated earlier have made clear, will do without the benefits of putative scientific precision.

5. *Meaningfulness.* I am tempted to claim that philosophic propositions may fruitfully be looked upon as a type of *performative utterance.* (This I derive as a speculative generalization from Hintikka's well-known analysis of Descartes's *cogito*).† However, if they are performative, philosophic dicta must be interpreted, in my view, as both *performative* and *injunctive*, and a wedding between these two categories involves large risks. A performative utterance, following J. L. Austin, is one that makes itself true (or the case) in being said (or done). Examples would be christenings, coronations, baptisms, marriage ceremonies, in all cases presupposing the competency, legitimacy, or qualifications of the people involved, and any other relevant background. I maintain, however, that philosophic assertions (or self-instantiating commands) do *not* make themselves true merely by being, as Descartes would say, "pronounced or mentally conceived." Mere entertainment in thought or speech is insufficient, though it may at times be necessary, as a condition for the realization of the imperatives that are embedded in genuinely philosophic pronouncements.

What, then, qualifies a statement as properly philosophic? Just this: that there is a direct manner in

†See below, n2.

which philosophic statements are *tested* or *validated*. That involves some form of *empirical corroboration*. I am not saying that philosophic statements are, or are like, scientific hypotheses. I am saying that they are *confirmed* or disconfirmed in an appropriately similar manner, one that is on a continuum with scientific modes of verification, though not identical therewith.

* What validates or invalidates a philosophic statement is whether or not its proponent ever actually carries out the command contained therein. I cannot put it more simply or emphatically than that.

* The test, then, of a philosophic utterance is whether or not the directive that it conceals or reveals is ultimately internalized or appropriated in the life of the individual putting the utterance forward. Execution is the touchstone of the norm's vitality, and of dedication to upholding it.

There are several noteworthy features of this approach. The remainder of this chapter will be devoted to sketching as many of them can be elicited from the theory. Note the following:

(a) It is still possible to maintain the performative-utterance view of philosophic statements, coordinate with the foregoing. Take the *cogito* as a test case: the French scholar Schrecker, for instance, once declared that the *cogito* was an empirical statement (in contradistinction to Kant, who throughout several polemics regards the *cogito* as a tautology, an analytic a priori judgment, therefore uninformative at best, and question-begging [because allegedly presupposing the existence of the external world] at worst). The *cogito* is true because, to put it bluntly, Descartes was, and because Descartes thought! (whether the connection between these two factual states of affairs is logical, causal, or "ontological" may be left open, since it does not directly concern us). I see nothing in Hintikka's express consideration of Schrecker's arguments that repudiates this strand in

the interpretation of the *cogito*; and, as Hintikka recognizes, the *cogito* is both temporally bound and exclusively
first-person singular in its own formulations, as well as in
the relevant truth-condition specifications that can be given
for it.[2] In this way, the *cogito* serves as a nice illustration of
one aspect of the thesis about philosophic utterances that I
have in mind, although I shall try, in the latter part of this
chapter, to adduce even better ones.

(b) It is now possible to take up again the criticism that I
lodged against the theory in its initial formulation: namely,
how are *deontological predictions* possible? They are possible just in the sense in which predictions generally may be
made. A prediction is true or false depending on whether
what it predicts does or does not occur. A deontological
prediction is subject to exactly the same constraints. *It is
true if and only if the command it issues is subsequently
obeyed by the agent issuing it.* If technical terminology
seems offensive, it is dispensable. I am no longer asking the
reader to suspend judgment, still less to abandon principles
or good sense sheerly for the momentary enjoyment that
may be brought about by recommending a novel way of
looking at philosophy. I *am* affirming that the theory as it
has just been expounded does stand up under examination,
and that it passes whatever test is made of it by conven-
tional logic and the ordinary standards of correct reasoning.
This is not to say that the theory is above criticism, only
that it can resist one particular criticism directed against it
earlier. On this issue I rest my case for the time being.

6. *Extensions.* I want next to develop some ramifications
of the theory of philosophic utterances just proposed. It
has, I think, several uses. It can be gainfully employed in

2. See K. J. J. Hintikka, "*Cogito, ergo sum:* Inference or Performance?"
Philosophical Review 71 (1962): 3-32. See also Hintikka's reply to critics, in *ibid.*
72 (1963): 487-96. For Kant's strictures on Descartes, see *Critique of Pure Reason,*
B274-75; A354-55; B422-23n.

the exegesis of philosophic texts, which is one very notable application. Moreover, it can be used to evaluate such writings for what will be called their philosophic content. In this way it serves simultaneously to distinguish philosophic from nonphilosophic *practice,* although the boundaries of underlying or corresponding *theories* will, in all likelihood, remain fuzzy and indistinct for all time. This explanation of the function of philosophic thought also enables the formation of a *relevance criterion:* a means for evaluating so-called philosophical problems and issues for their genuineness. Of this more will be said later.

The reader will no doubt detect one serious and apparent flaw in the above presentation. If philosophic utterances are to be both normative and cognitive, then in virtue of the kinds of procedures just outlined (see esp. the two asterisked statements above), there must be an inexpungeably *biographical,* even *auto*biographical, element pertaining to each and every would-be philosophic assertion. The question is: is this a flaw? Not as I see it! I want to suggest that the life of a philosopher bears an intrinsic and important relationship to the philosophic status of his work and ideas; indeed, it can have a *philosophically* decisive bearing thereon. The theory does not merely commit me to this view indirectly, for this outlook is an integral part of the theory, and one I embrace wholeheartedly. This fragment of the theory captures my intentions exactly.

The pertinent question then is shifted: if the theory is accurate, who qualifies as a philosopher? And the answer is: very few people, even fewer than the small number generally accorded such status. I shall say this as unceremoniously as possible: a distinction should be drawn between *philosophers* and *theoreticians.* There is no shame in being a theoretician; some of the greatest minds, St. Thomas, Leibniz, Aristotle, and Hegel among them, have been theorizers of the highest order. But, even in a spirit of utmost generosity and anti-dogmatism, I cannot say that they were philosophers. Plato, Plotinus, Pascal, Kant, Augustine, and Spinoza, on the other hand, do qualify, among others, for this title, under the conditions set up: namely, that a man's life embody the principles he espouses, and/or that the ideas for which he achieves renown in some way encapsulate the course of his personal struggle to achieve stability.

Those who abhor such an approach for involving an unmistakable *ad hominem* should simply stop reading. I prefer to conceive of it as distinctly *pro homine*, but that is another matter. I am by no means inclined to denigrate the accomplishments of theoreticians, to deny that they merit prolonged study, or to hold that they are inferior to other human productions. Nor would I claim that one cannot be both a skilled theorizer and a philosopher; and although it is exceedingly difficult to unite both sets of qualities as well as their respective temperaments in one and the same individual, it can be done, and it has been (Parmenides, if the ancient historical legends about him are correct, might qualify as the first representative of both traditions). What I am calling attention to is sometimes referred to and thereby distinguished under the suggestive but inadequate labels of "wisdom" *vs.* "knowledge."[3] The two functions are complementary, not mutually opposed; nevertheless, there is a significant difference between them, which the (auto-) biographical criterion brings out sharply.

The problem with the requirement for the testability of a philosophic utterance is *not* its defiance of intellectual impersonality. It is rather one of establishing a biographical terminus for the evaluation of philosophic statements. In

3. A related, but not equivalent, series of distinctions between 'theorogon' and 'pathologon' philosophers is brilliantly drawn, in a genetic framework, by Felix M. Cleve in the Introduction to his *The Giants of Pre-Sophistic Greek Philosophy* (The Hague: Martinus Nijhoff, 1965).

one formulation I deliberately employed the word "ulti-mately" to refer to the time of appropriation. This leaves a loophole that I should now like to close. A philosopher who lived as a rogue only to perform deathbed recantations would no more have earned his life-spurs than a non-philosopher. There must be a clear trend (or else a sudden reversal, followed by an uninterrupted pattern of fidelity, as in Augustine's case) of growth or development that reveals continued devotion and adherence to some ideal, guiding principle, or set of norms. (There is nothing to prevent that ideal from being purely contemplative or conceptual in character, and its realization from taking place purely in the "realm of the mind": that is *one* way in which the theoreti-cian can be transformed into the philosopher and occupies both roles at once.)

The putative norms must themselves, it would appear, pass muster independently; or need they? A life lived in ac-cordance, say, with the ideals set forth in *On Liberty* would differ so dramatically from one faithful to the precepts of *Mein Kampf* that a comparison and evaluation of the two could be carried out simply by direct inspection (of type and quality of respective demeanors), and would demand nothing more (or less) than investigation into the examined individual's behavior. The norm would not, then, have to exist or be judged antecedently to its incorporation in some person's way of life; indeed, the norm's formulation could well emerge as a by-product of *living* that kind of life, its validity confirmed or disconfirmed by that life; for the two might interpenetrate, in complete, matching, one-to-one correspondence. The fact that, in the examples I chose, a work recommends a particular mode of conduct to ev-eryone, or to many others, is not accidental, yet the work is itself the result (for good or ill) of personal reflection coupled with presumed decision-making and subsequent action by its writer and originator. One can certainly act in deference to or in accordance with certain standards without consciously following their articulation and espousal by some predecessor, just as, analogously, it is certainly possible to be a good Christian without ever reading the Bible.[4] The explicit framing of rules for the purpose of guidance is nothing if it is not derivative from the lessons taught by human, personal experience, and, equally significantly, if such general rules as may be framed are to be adequate and sound ones, they must be framed in light of such personal experience as may accrue to their framer.

It will be observed, then, that one's theory can be flexible as well as impartial in judging individual character, but that there is required loyalty to some (moral, religious, political, or other) ideal, loyalty that is *not* vacillating, discontinuous, just a momentary affair. The ideal need not be a preexistent one; but more important even than its being created or verbally formulated by the thinker in question is its being *self-imposed* and binding on the proponent of it. Universality is an inessential component of this; personal commitment is what is uppermost.

What this amounts to is a *sincerity-criterion:* a philosophic espousal is genuine if and only if it is taken up in the philosopher's life and remains part of it for some length of time, and supports him through various crises; for practice of what one preaches may *not* be merely episodic, *unless* the episodes assume apocalyptic dimensions, in which case they very probably end the individual's human career! That the lines to be drawn cannot be drawn finely is no indication that they cannot be drawn at all. I must appeal to the reader's intuition in support of this.

The reader may object at this point that, on the theory

4. J. S. Mill's example; see *Utilitarianism*, chap. 2. Of course, one can always read the Bible and be a bad Christian, but this is tantamount to being no Christian at all. Similarly, one can be a "good Nazi"—but a good Nazi is a bad human being. That neatly disposes of the most obvious class of counter-examples.

proposed, countless people may qualify as philosophers. Indeed they may. But to demand practice consonant with (self-) preaching, is to presuppose or assume that one does preach. And this not everyone does. I said before that the articulation of a philosophic way of life is secondary to its being lived, but in being secondary it is not thereby relegated to negligible status. The intellectual component of the philosophic life is the other side of the same coin, and furnishes the material wherewith we corroborate all verbalizations and professions of faith with their personal embodiment in the life of their articulator. This half of the criterion eliminates those countless unknowns as candidates; they may stand to posterity as good men, and there is no small merit in that, but the title "philosopher" is to be withheld or reserved for a special sort of life-occupation.

It also goes without saying that an individual may sincerely change his mind, and therefore his life (or vice versa); St. Augustine is the classic example. This in no way weakens or nullifies the demands made in any of the above formulations.

7. *The philosopher and the multitude.* I said above that philosophic imperatives are "singulary." How does this accord with my admission that the philosopher in effect is a teacher, a moral or spiritual leader, a representative of (or candidate for) the "wisdom-tradition," or a preacher—at any rate, someone who addresses others? The reply here is two-fold: first, in being singulary, philosophic dicta apply (like the *cogito*) to one person *at a time*, or *ad seriatem*. They are true even when true universally because they are absorbed into the lives of individuals one by one, and are assimilated accordingly. (This does not commit me to a kind of political or social atomism.) If this reply seems unsatisfactory, or trivial, I might amend it simply by reverting to the "practice what you preach" slogan. The second consideration is therefore the elementary and related one of taking

steps to insist that the philosopher practice what he preaches *before* he ever begins preaching it *to others*. One lingering aspect of the performative-utterance version of the theory (justifiably) intrudes itself at this point: ideally, philosophic utterances play a role in *goading* their *originators* in a manner that (temporally) antedates their possible rhetorical role in persuading or exhorting others. In either case, we may desire to replace the performative-utterance thesis, whose inadequacies, taken in isolation, have already been reviewed, with a much subtler modification of the awkwardly conjoined performative-injunctive theory: on this new thesis, philosophic utterances are *protreptic* in character, and, in the first instance, self-protreptic (just as they are self-prescriptive, self-instantiating, and so forth).

There is a difficulty with this, in that it mitigates the effect of my very first stipulation, namely, that philosophic utterances must be future-tensed. On the latest construal, a philosopher (or a would-be, aspiring philosopher) has no "right," so to speak, to give advice to others until and unless he has taken his own advice seriously.[5] In that case, the pragmatic test for meaningfulness of a philosophic assertion (command though it be, but one with declarative equivalents) would already have been conducted, not once and for all but certainly in a provisional manner, in the *past!* How do we reconcile this with the insistence on the future as the dimension for the realization of norms promulgated by philosophic insight?

I believe there are two approaches that may be taken. One is, to modify the *predictive* requirement in a harmless way by pointing out that the realization of norms is always a progressive or at least an ongoing matter, so that whatever

5. Philosophers as diverse as Sartre and Nowell-Smith sometimes contend that philosophic advice-giving is either impossible or else immoral; however, I shall pass over their arguments in silence, since they do not concern self-prescription.

incomplete ground has been prepared for it in the life of
the individual is nothing compared to what its furtherance
or perpetuation may ask of him; indeed, to what he asks of
himself, if he be a true philosopher. A second, and again
related, way to overcome the difficulty is through maintaining that realization of a norm is always an "approximate"
matter,[6] and therefore is never fully reached. One appeals
then to keenly felt and widely shared human frustration
which the pursuit of goals nearly always implies, even when
our aspirations encounter no insuperable obstacles standing
in the way of achieving both eventual consummation and
resulting (or attendant) satisfaction. The philosopher is in no
way exempt from having such feelings, or from noting the
imperfect state of accomplishment they bespeak. The
asymptotic quality of action and the restraints exercised by
nonsuccess illustrate very nicely the problem of harmoniz-
ing past with future through the medium of the present (so
that the philosophic reformulation of life standards is, one
must suppose, perpetually taking place).

8. *Philosophy and nonphilosophy.* We are now in a position to redeem the pledge wherein I claimed that the
theory of philosophic assertion outlined in this essay could
be of assistance in identifying philosophy and providing
criteria of merit for it. Here the sense of "philosophy" I
have in mind is honorific, and restricted to the kind of intrinsically valuable undertaking already described, namely,
the *discovery or invention of systematic and mutual correla-
tions between intellect and character,* which activity serves
as its own justification. About this sufficient preparatory
elucidation has already taken place above. If the reader follows (and approves of) our method and procedure, it should
then be easy to cite some examples of lives (not necessarily

---

6. This term is borrowed from Kierkegaard, but his use of it is considerably
different from my own, as are the grounds on which it is introduced by SK in the
Postscript.

heroic ones, although doubtless admirable, since one good reason for making philosophic utterances first-person relative is to prevent supererogatory acts from being translated into individual duties, immediately or prematurely), lives that embody and incorporate the ideals of the life of uprightness and wisdom, be they spiritual, contemplative, or of whatever specific sort. Anyone may draw up his own list, and readily see from it that the desired personal fulfillment of these ideals, however fragmentary or partial, is in each case unduplicable and unique, but not for that reason any less worthy of commendation, as representing wisdom at its best.

Nor does the presence of diversity mean that there is no underlying philosophic uniformity, that is, that the personages one selects have nothing in common; if that were the case, the method of selection would be at fault, or else the criteria would have been inconsistently and incongruously applied. I am, however, quite prepared to demonstrate that, upon recital of names of eminent philosophers, important family resemblances can always be detected (say, between Erasmus and Berkeley, united in their opposition to cant, pedantry, and obfuscation). This is also true of attempts to bring all philosophers (including various representatives of the knowledge tradition) "under one roof," and should therefore encourage, not deter us.

Rather than recount outstanding philosophical personalities (not to mention a few highly questionable ones!), I should like to point out how the theory of philosophic utterances permits us to *differentiate* between true philosophy and theoretical inquiry. Take an issue that is buring in contemporary "analytic" thought: the notion of referential opacity, due to Quine. Now in what way is referential opacity amenable to the kind of treatment that the foregoing theory of philosophic utterances lays down? I submit, in *no way whatsoever*. The same is true (across the

board) for so-called philosophic problems such as the new
riddle of induction, the ontological status of number, the
existence of sense-data, and a range of others. One must be
technically proficient, indeed very adept, to deal responsibly with these issues and others like them; but they neither
require philosophical acumen nor do they directly encourage or coax it into being. (And these talents are certainly
not coextensive, either, if the reader is in agreement with
me up to this point). In addition, the perceptive observer of
contemporary thought may concur that not a few erstwhile
dilemmas that even today might conceivably, in some setting, qualify as genuinely philosophical under proper conditions for the formulation and implementation of responses
to them, usually are handled in a way such as to place them
at several removes from philosophy (the mind-body problem, and the raging controversy over "existence" as a logical term being two pertinent examples), or at any rate far
from previous and recognizably philosophic contexts (the
concept of Self, the purported demonstration of God's existence, etc.). Philosophy can thus become a sheerly technical enterprise. It is not my intention to protest or complain
here about this "degeneration" of a once-noble activity. I
am content not to associate myself with such humbug, and
to explain, in the process of so doing, why I am not at all
perturbed by the "failure" of the theory of philosophic utterances as set forth here to encompass *mere* and remote
technicalities as they are exhibited, say, in certain current
academic trends.

Philosophy at the hands of its theorizing "predators" has
its own rationale and, in the contemporary climate, its
motivations, which are all easy enough to discern and therefore not part of my purpose either to deplore or explore. It
is enough if the theory of philosophic utterances propounded here enables us to *distinguish* between gold and
dross. It furnishes us, in effect, with a *significance-criterion*

for the *evaluation* of philosophic doctrines and tenets; for if they address themselves to sheerly intellectual conundrums that have or bear no *conceivable,* no rescuable relation, direct or otherwise, to the identity, personality, and general mode of conduct of the *inquirer,* then they are to be considered as either nonphilosophic, or, slightly more charitably, philosophic but quite low on the scale of importance.

It is worthwhile to emphasize that this judgment can be made quite dispassionately. It is likewise to be noted that I do not mean to screech in the dark about "relevance," nor to foster despisal of and contempt for legitimate forms of intellectual endeavor. Further, consider that each person casts himself in the role of inquirer in determining for himself whether (for whatever reasons) the beginning (or the continuation) of some line of investigation is personally profitable or meritorious. Therefore, the just-mentioned significance-criterion does become "universal," perfectly general in the potential scope of its application, but once more, only *ad seriatem.* This is *not* merely an incidental fact about the momentary state of mind of the originator of the problem, topic, theme, or dispute. To ask whether Quine qualifies as a philosopher in my sense (the answer is obviously, no) is one thing; to ask it of oneself, when one is beginning to immerse oneself in "Quinoid quibbles,"[7] is central and of far-reaching consequence.

9. *Good and bad philosophy.* On my theory, if I may call it that, bad philosophy is either philosophy that for some reason fails to make itself manifest in the life of its proponents, or else is a philosophy that leads to a life distinguished for its lack of distinction, if not for more positively adverse qualities. A philosophy may fail to realize itself [8] in

---

7. I owe this term to John B. Bacon, who, I am sure, does not concur with my derogatory usage of it.

8. I am aware that my language here (as before) is, broadly speaking, Hegelian, and I am happy to acquiesce in that, for the time being.

the life of its originator or guiding spirit for several reasons: error; moral weakness; an improbable standard, inhuman or superhuman in its demands; external barriers and obstacles; defects in its intellectual articulation; and the like. These failures exemplify an array of causes familiar to all ethical theorists, so I shall not rehearse them at length. The fact that a man may not live up to an ideal is, as Locke well expressed it, proof against the man, not against the feasibility of the ideal. The sincerity-criterion is more frequently violated by just that—by hypocrisy—than by anything else. But, as I have observed, anyone can (and indeed must) put himself in the place of the philosopher, and imagine or conceptualize himself as the inquirer, and then try to live up to that standard. This in turn means that the initial failure of the experiment, including the fragmentary thought-experiment, is not conclusive testimony against either the workability or the genuineness of the norm being considered.

Nonphilosophy, by contrast, is that which could be neither good nor bad philosophy. It stands to philosophy in just the same way as (cognitively) meaningless statements stand to true and false ones. On my definition, most of the problems that occupy contemporary philosophers are non-philosophical; and correspondingly, they are not philosophers, whatever their other accomplishments. This is not because of any personal drawbacks, but is owing to the sheerly technical character of so much of the work that is being done; today this effectively *precludes* philosophy from manifesting itself, or even from finding a seedbed to nourish itself during an uncreative interim. I shall not press this polemic, for I think its main features are by now threateningly obvious!

If we wish to accord the designation "philosopher" only to good (or great) philosophers, instead of applying it generically to a wider class of cases, that would not meet with any objection here; it is analogous to the somewhat controversial practice of calling only great art "art." The perils of either policy are enormous, and one is no more fraught with them than the other. We need not delve into that matter any more deeply, either.

II

10. *Paradigms.* Consider the following claim: "virtue is knowledge." Now, what does this mean? Let us dissect the sentence systematically:

(i) virtue = human excellence, specifically "all-around" moral and political excellence, on the model of excellence in some art, skill, or craft, but far more general in scope

(ii) Knowledge = a combination of practical wisdom and temperance or self-control, enabling its possessor to judge the desirability of ends, the chances for obtaining them, the fitness of means (to be) utilized to acquire the desired object or attain the desired result, and the opportune or correct time to put plans for reaching the desired goal into operation

(iii) "virtue is knowledge" has several possible meanings.[9] It could mean (a) that virtue=knowledge, that the two terms are synonymous; (b) that virtue and knowledge are extensionally (referentially) equivalent; whoever has one, possesses the other; (c) that virtue is *part* of knowledge, knowledge being a wider concept that *includes* virtue.

9. For full study, see M. J. O'Brien, *The Socratic Paradoxes and the Greek Mind* (Chapel Hill, N.C.: University of North Carolina Press, 1967); also W. K. C. Guthrie, *Socrates* (Cambridge: Cambridge University Press, 1971), esp. pp. 130-39. I cannot agree with the grossly undervaluing interpretation offered by Gulley in *The Philosophy of Socrates* (London and New York: Methuen, 1968), esp. pp. 165ff.

Any of these proposals suffices to render intelligble the use of the formula "virtue is knowledge" in its context. But then, none of them really captures what Socrates meant, nor explains why he labored so strenuously, both in *Protagoras* and *Meno*, to demonstrate by his own example *the teachability* of virtue, as well as boldly to maintain the highly counter-intuitive thesis that no man does evil voluntarily.[10] The Socratic conviction is that "to know self-control is to practice it,"[11] or more simply, that *to know the good is (means) to be good.* (Doubtless Socrates would affirm the converse, too. For one cannot be virtuous without the necessary intellectual skills that enable deliberation to be carried out successfully. One may, as Aristotle would say, uncoercedly perform virtuous *acts*, but they can only happen strictly by accident or chance, not as due to choices that are themselves the product of rational forethought; they would be unlikely to recur, and would not promote any settled convictions or even habits of right-doing.)

"To know the good is to be good." What does this mean? It means that knowledge that does not become implemented in moral practice is not worthy of the name, is not full-blooded, is not knowledge at all, at least not in that sense of "knowledge" involving practical wisdom. It also means that anyone who does know the good, in the fullest sense just specified, is *automatically* good (assuming he is not "morally paralyzed"[12]), or is drawn to do the good as irresistibly as staples are to a magnet. He never becomes a victim of temptation, for his only temptation is to *be* good,

10. Aristotle is often fingered as one who held up the data of human frailty and experience against both Socrates and Plato on this point. But Aristotle's own account of *akrasia* is in some respects remarkably close to his two predecessors in its tone. See J. Walsh, *Aristotle's Conception of Moral Weakness* (New York: Columbia University Press, 1963).

11. J. H. Randall, Jr., *Plato: Dramatist of the Life of Reason* (New York: Columbia University Press, 1970), p. 155.

12. See my paper "The Logic of Moral Paralysis," *Journal of Value Inquiry* 8 (1973): 61-64.

and it is one he indulges freely; it is also the one inclination he *need* not resist. His actions are not without their own affective pathology, but his conduct and the course of his life alike reveal an intellectual maturity behind the emotional exuberance of his good deeds, one that exercises responsibility and takes firm control at every moment, and "steers the throttle" of his soul. He is the model of the moral man.

Whom can we name who is like this? Who is capable of integrating intellectual *and* moral virtue into a whole? Whose very life exhibits a harmony of this sort? Socrates, and only Socrates, qualifies on all counts. (The unspoken tragedy of the dialogues is that he never found a suitable partner.) He knows the good, in spite of his professions of ignorance,[13] and he does the good; and the *relationship* between his knowledge of the good and his goodness is, again, one of causal, logical, and psychological *interpenetration;* they are thoroughly fused in his person, each feeding, informing, and reinforcing the other. Aristotle observed that the object of the moral life is not to know the good so much as to *be* good, but this implies a separability (if only for purposes of reasoned analysis) that Socrates, for one, emphatically repudiates. It is this *kind* of rejection, coupled with the example that Socrates sets as a man, that marks the difference between himself and an Aristotle; between the philosopher (man of wisdom) and the theorizer, contemplator, or knower (in a different, yet more refined sense of the term "knowledge" than that allied with "virtue").

Admittedly, Socrates is a heroic example, perhaps one too difficult to even hope to emulate, but we must remember that the sole portrait of his life and character that the *Dialogues* allow us to ferret out is a highly idealized and dramatized one. Nevertheless, he does serve very admira-

13. For full study, see E. G. Ballard, *Socratic Ignorance* (The Hague: Martinus Nijhoff, 1968), and W. K. C. Guthrie, *Socrates,* esp. pp. 122-29.

bly in his capacity as the embodiment of the norms contained in the heretical slogan "virtue is knowledge," to support the philosophic-utterance thesis as it has been propounded. In addition, "Socratism" fulfills our expectation of an illustration to (as it were) supersede the *cogito,* and in so doing, renders the thesis both more compelling and less austere.

It may finally be objected that what I have been doing up to now is detailing, not a linguistic theory about philosophy, but a churlish piece of arrant legislation, dictated entirely by extra-linguistic factors. That the theory presented is normative, it would be foolish to deny; that the linguistic aspects of it are tailored by some personal conceptions of the proper tasks of philosophy, is at least better than to have it the other way around. So once more, criticisms must yield, not to Mill's "dissolving force of analysis," but before the rebuttal that once-seeming defects turn into advantages when vices appear, under a different light, as virtues.

There is this much truth in the critique, that the leading considerations in the formulation of my proposal are not adopted from some other discipline but are internal to philosophy, no matter how widely or narrowly we interpret the domain comprised by it. I said at the outset that a full-blown theory about philosophy, which is what we now have on our hands, is both unavoidable and undesirable to avoid; those contentions have, I think, been borne out. The linguistic apparatus takes its bearings from my philosophical themes, but this is only as it should be. I should only be sorry to learn (what may undeniably be the case) that the rules, at least as formulated, are incomplete, or that they suffer from legalistic defects. The theory, as mentioned at the beginning, makes no claim to comprehensiveness, but I would urge and argue that what and where it does summarize, it does adequately, and that in spirit it *is* complete for what it purports to describe, even if in letter it is beset by formal gaps or other shortcomings.

11. *Historical antecedents.* I conclude with some discussion of the views of Kierkegaard, which, as stated in the introduction, inspired the present essay. Many of the ideas entertained here find their expression in an unfinished, unpublished, and pseudonymous fragment by this enigmatic and elusive author.[14] It would therefore be idle to attempt to settle whether they are Kierkegaard's own considered opinion or not. Fortunately, there is no need to determine whether the views of the narrator correspond to those of either the author (SK) or the subject (Johannes Climacus) of this biographical romance, this intellectual odyssey entitled *De Omnibus Dubitandum Est.* This is because SK has (deliberately) made it impossible, and mistaken in principle,[15] to attempt to decide the question of attribution. Scholars who are still pursuing this gambit have been attracted by the wrong calling. In any case we are indebted to SK for a masterful excursion in the vexed area of methodology in the historiography of ideas,[16] and for present purposes, nothing else really counts.

In *De Omnibus*, Johannes Climacus is portrayed as a young student struggling to come to grips with the prevailing dogmas of modern thought. In particular, he attempts to think through Cartesian "methodic doubt" for himself, and he reaches the following, always aporetic conclusions:[17]

14. S. Kierkegaard, *Johannes Climacus: or, De Omnibus Dubitandum Est, and A Sermon,* trans. T. H. Croxall (Stanford, Calif.: 1958).

15. This is one of many cogent conclusions emanating from the masterful study by L. Mackey, *Kierkegaard: A Kind of Poet* (Philadelphia: University of Pennsylvania Press, 1971).

16. To be sure, the work contains the germs of later inquiries, both in the *Postscript* and in the *Fragments,* into the relation between inner, personal belief and the status of Christianity conceived as a historical, temporal sequence of dramatic events. SK's indirect lessons on other phil-historical problems show every sign of being wholly unintentional, but they are there, nonetheless.

17. Kierkegaard, *De Omnibus Dubitandum Est,* esp. pp. 116, 119, 121, 122, 131, 133-34, 136, 142, 152, 153.

(1) If philosophy must begin in the manner that Descartes prescribed, then no philosophers prior to Descartes (and few thereafter) were really philosophers after all. This seems intolerant to the past, especially if Descartes himself is willing to accept the consequences. However, equally disturbingly,

(2) If we weaken the claim, to say instead that *modern* philosophy must start from doubt, then we are no longer putting forward a strictly philosophical proposition, but instead resorting to mere doxography. Even so, to be in a position to discriminate between modern philosophy and previous modes of thought presupposes some philosophical judgments; in particular, why is the appearance of methodic doubt considered so decisive for philosophy as to mark a turning point? Moreover, what (besides rampant eclecticism) permits us to assimilate Cartesian thought to the older traditions (and vice versa), and to put each on the same plateau by calling them "philosophy" alike?

(3) If Descartes had not existed, the project of methodic doubt would have had no founder (*N.B.*, SK would certainly dismiss the crude version of historical determinism according to which "If Descartes had not come along, someone else performing the same function would have done so eventually"). So Descartes's presence is irreplaceable. Yet he counsels mankind to accept nothing on authority, but only on the testimony of their own reason. Yet, without Descartes, this elevation of autonomous reason would be quite powerless to start itself. The paradox, then, is that if we attempt to follow Descartes's advice, we cannot generate any philosophical doctrines; yet if we read Descartes, we are submitting ourselves to *his* tenets, not merely his regimen; and in *either* case, we are accepting *his* word as authority, instead of submitting everything (including Descartes's own statements) before the bar of reason; and "everything" would include the revolutionary proposal to methodically doubt everything (yet another paradox).

To resolve this entire puzzle,[18] Kierkegaard asks himself, under the consistent guise of Johannes's reminiscences of student days, whether Descartes might not stand to later philosophers in a relation similar to that of Christ's relationship to mankind: "perhaps one philosopher has doubted for all," exactly as Christ (or Thales?) suffered for all our sins, thereby making it *unnecessary* to repeat the process. Philosophy, then, begins with doubt, but begins so for Descartes *alone*, while for the rest of mankind, philosophy requires for an initiation only the belief (or the faith) "that philosopher So-and-So has doubted for him."[19] Tracing the steps taken by Descartes becomes superfluous (it may also exhibit unbridled *hybris*, if such comparison is apt; after all, a Descartes complex and, say, a Christ complex would not be so far apart).

But then doubt has turned into dogmatic assurance, and Descartes's warning about authority *vs.* reason has receded into the background; it is ignored in favor of adopting the remainder of his theories. This sort of neglect is not benign; for methodic doubt is not merely one commandment among many, but the most fundamental of all of them. Moreover, as SK very well realizes, it is methodic doubt that supposedly yields, if anything can, the *cogito;*[20] and from the *cogito, all* of the other vital theories and assumptions of Descartes's philosophy are in turn produced. So, to allow Descartes to methodically doubt "for" us is a little like allowing *Hamlet* to be performed without the main character.

18. It is one that arises in part from a failure to take seriously one's obligations (if any) to one's audience or public. The *only* major philosopher to consider the logic of this relation explicitly is Hegel, in certain sections of the Preface to the *Phenomenology;* several undercurrents of it are found occuring sporadically in Plato, Kant, and other writers as well.

19. *De Omnibus*, p. 137; see also p. 119. This kind of vicarious doubt might be preferable to some, but it is inconsistent with Descartes's own skepticism and zest for mental self-reliance, both fundamental to his outlook.

20. This is eloquently reasoned out in Heinrich Scholz, "Ueber das Cogito, ergo sum," *Kant-Studien* 36 (1931): 126-47, who shows that the *cogito* is a generalization from and expansion of the *dubito* (and see Descartes, *Principles of Philosophy*, 1:7).

It is too basic a step to be skipped; there are no substitutes for it, and there is no way to plunge into Descartes *in medias res* and still expect to regain the thread of the inquiry later, if doubt is dropped.

In addition, is it or is it not possible to doubt methodically without reaching the particular conclusions that Descartes (sometimes spuriously, or with insufficient warrant) establishes? If so, then one is taking Descartes's authority *as* authority just so far, and no further. What right has one to depart from the sole available paradigm of methodic doubt, in evident ingratitude? More to the point, *how* can one even do so, once one has agreed to surrender one's reason to Cartesianism in order to escape from the phil-historical paradoxes depicted above? If reason is powerless to get underway without methodic doubt, from where does it obtain its ability to challenge or question the inquiry at any juncture subsequent to its launching?

From considerations such as these, Climacus is moved to jettison his entire effort to master modern philosophy as learned from his academic masters. Dissatisfied with the ineffective, half-baked methodology and the insufferable consequences of the poor models of correct philosophic discourse that surround him, he is led to ask the key, the headlining question: "what is the attitude of the propounder of our sentence to the sentence he propounds?"[21] He thereupon formulates his own alternative theory of philosophical discourse. The passage in which he does so should be quoted *in extenso*, with occasional interruptions for notes and commentary:

> With this quest in mind, J. C. asked whether the principle that philosophy begins with doubt had in the temporal sense existed through all ages, so that everybody knew its content even though nobody had explicitly

21. *De Omnibus*, p. 134.

stated its terms. Had it the same validity as the sentence "Man is mortal"? Did it but state something that people in all ages had done without being conscious of it? And was this action something which is inherent in human nature, like wonder, for example? For if nobody had ever explained what it is to wonder, every single person nevertheless would wonder.

SK's strategy here depends upon distinguishing between truths that are independent of human apprehension, and those that come into play only thanks to the emergence of conscious reflection.

> Or had the principle that philosophy begins with doubt existed through all ages in the eternal sense, but yet had not been discovered in time? Had it the same validity as mathematical propositions, which, when they are discovered, are discovered in their infinity? Would the principle continue to exist in the eternal sense through all ages, just as a philosophic truth does? Was the personality of the discoverer of the principle unaffected by his discovery, as is the case with mathematical and metaphysical principles?[22]

Now Kierkegaard is able to border on the explicit introduction of another crucial distinction, that between personal and impersonal truths, one that is useful both in corroborating assertions and in examining the active workability of a proposed course of conduct or basic "life-style":

> Was it of importance for the principle that one should know the personality of the man who propounded it? With religious principles, we certainly insist on having some knowledge of the speaker's personality; so also, to a certain extent, with ethical principles. For anybody can utter a religious or ethical principle, but it does not fol-

22. The tension between "eternal philosophy" and historically conditioned study is brought out elsewhere; see *De Omnibus*, pp. 119, 131, 137.

low that in everyone's mouth it becomes a religious or
ethical principle, unless we suppose, for example, that it
is of no importance who said he was the Son of God—
Christ or anybody else; or that it is of no importance who
said "Know thyself"—whether it was a man who really
knew himself or anybody else. The statement certainly
continues the same, and yet it becomes different. That is
to say, in the one case it was a principle, in the other,
chatter; whereas with a mathematical proposition it is entirely a matter of indifference whether it is Archimedes
or tradition that propounds the proposition, so only it be
propounded rightly. Personality in the one case means
nothing, in the other, everything; just as in civil life no
one can be, in the formal sense, a guarantor, and yet it
makes all the difference who the guarantor is.

Next, Kierkegaard addresses himself to the inevitable
question of formulating truth-criteria for testing personal utterances embodying (claimed) wisdom:

What then must be the kind of personality possessed
by one who propounds this proposition? Must he have talent, and is this sufficient, so that if only he has talent he
has authority to propound our proposition?[23] To state a
mathematical proposition, mathematical talent is required. He who can state it rightly, shows that he has
the talent. And if we can imagine the absurd situation
that a person without talent could propound a mathematical proposition (which is for ever an absurdity because
the very propounding implies complete immanent possession of talent), the proposition would still retain its
truth, its mathematical truth, i.e. its essential truth; just
as in ordinary life a bond payable to bearer is just as
valid whether a rich man or a poor man is the payee,
whether it is a thief or its rightful owner who possesses
it.

23. By "talent" SK means, as the subsequent remarks indicate, something akin
to "intellectual ability and gifts." One may wish to compare it with Aristotle's notion of "quick wit" and apprehension, in *Posterior Analytics*, or Spinoza's third and
highest kind of knowledge ("intuition") in the *Ethics*.

Once again SK reiterates what he has just clarified:

> With religious and ethical propositions this is not the
> case. If one could teach a child of two a mathematical
> proposition, or if a madman stated it, it would be essen-
> tially just as true in the mouth of the child or madman as
> in the mouth of Pythagoras. But if one were to teach a
> child of two to say "I believe in the existence of God," or
> "Know thyself," nobody would take him seriously. For
> the fact is that if religious and ethical statements[24] are to
> have any meaning, authority must inhere in them.

The rhetoric of intensely inner "authority" reinforces the
idea that *content* and *character* cannot be divorced in framing genuinely philosophical judgments; that to do so invites
the reduction of philosophy to mathematics, or some other
"objective" discipline:

> Should then the person who propounds our
> philosophical sentence likewise have authority? Or is ta-
> lent itself sufficient authority?[25] In order to propound a
> philosophical thesis,[26] philosophical talent is sufficient au-
> thorization. But with religious and ethical truths, some-
> thing else is required, another sort of authority, some-
> thing you can really call authority. For there is a differ-
> ence between talent and authority. If a person has suffi-
> cient talent to see all the implications of a religious or
> ethical thesis, and talent enough to present it, it does not
> follow that he himself believes it, or himself performs it.
> And if this is not the case, then he commutes the propos-

24. As opposed, e.g., to empirically scientific statements, including objectively
historical ones.

25. By "authority" SK means neither subjective assurance nor the mere conviction of infallibility stemming from long first-hand acquaintance with the materials
of some intellectual pursuit. He means instead something equivalent to being "in
the state of grace," thanks to having managed to incorporate one's "sentence" or
principle in one's life ("to be what one says," quoted by Croxall, *De Omnibus*, p.
135n1).

26. SK implicitly refers to Hegel's "System," or any other pretended scientific
(metaphysical) accounts of reality. "Authority" can never be impersonal, let alone
institutional.

ition from a religious to a historical one, or from an ethical to a metaphysical one.

So armed, SK returns to the Cartesian dilemma that confronted his protagonist at the outset:

> Now as we have seen, J. C. had become convinced that there cannot be four beginnings to philosophy.[27] Even if there had been, his conclusion would be the same, viz. that the statement "Philosophy begins with doubt" must come under the heading of a subjective beginning. This is also clear from the fact that it is sheer nonsense to speak of an objective doubt; for objective doubt is not doubt but deliberation.[28] The proposition therefore "Philosophy begins with doubt" cannot, any more than any other philosophical proposition, lay claim to mathematical necessity; neither can it lay claim to philosophical necessity,[29] as do all propositions in absolute and objective philosophy. This statement "Philosophy begins with doubt" must therefore be such that whoever propounds it, must have talent, must have authority.[30]

In other words, whoever says that philosophy begins with doubt must also *live* his philosophy. (If he cannot, then perhaps someone else can.) That imperative also furnishes the test for the *meaningfulness* (as SK himself recalcitrantly phrases it) of "ethical and religious" propositions, which I have widened in this presentation to encompass philosophi-

27. *De Omnibus*, p. 116, on three respective formulations of the Cartesian first principle of (or the indispensable preliminary for) philosophizing, plus the overall "subjective beginning" mentioned in the following sentence.

28. For which notion, along with more discussion on the "four beginnings of philosophy," see *De Omnibus*, pp. 133-34. (Compare, in this connection, C. S. Peirce's later criticism of Cartesianism as highly disingenuous, in the famous 1868 papers on capacities claimed for man.)

29. SK is again thinking of the pretensions of Hegelian dialectic, although one need not limit oneself to this convenient example.

30. *De Omnibus*, pp. 134-36. For an illustration of the personal authority that SK has in mind (his own father's), see *De Omnibus*, p. 110. Cf. also St. Augustine's doctrine of truth in *Confessions*, Bk. XI, chap. 3.

cal declarations generally. It is also the means whereby
their truth or falsity is reliably ascertained, as we examine
what happens when somebody does try to live by his own
assertions (which SK looks upon as tantamount to a creed)
or to evaluate the outcome. The truth-conditions for a
philosophical statement are then vastly different from those
germane to history, mathematics, or anything else; and this
shows how we can generically *distinguish* philosophy from
those other enterprises. This passage from SK tells its own
story, and it does so with such pointed eloquence that to
dare to recapitulate it would be in effect to retrace the entire ground already covered and defended in this chapter.

As observed a while back, those who find every type of
ad hominem approach repulsive should not continue reading, or at least should not be surprised to have encountered
the foregoing arguments. The theorist's tendency to separate person from cherished thesis is as old as the demands
once made by the unscrupulous Thrasymachus,[31] and yet
its merits are patent and are not to be gainsaid. Otherwise,
one could not plausibly maintain that a philosophic "guide
to life" is not refuted merely by a (philosopher's) personal
failure or refusal to put it into operation. Nevertheless, if I
have managed to make it abundantly clear by now that
there is some strong (and justifiable) relation between
philosophy and what SK calls "personality," and that mutual
imputations from each side have earned their rightful place
in the field, regardless of possible *abuses* of such biographical prerogative, then the entire effort has *not* been wasted.

12. *Motivation.* My overriding purpose in this chapter
(see the introduction, above) has been to arrive at a vision
of philosophy that could be unpacked through certain preliminary formalizations and technical considerations: considerations always and solely in the *service* of that vision as it

---

31. See *Republic* 349A. For commentary, see F. E. Sparshott, "Socrates and
Thrasymachus," *The Monist* 50 (1966): 458, n50.

worked itself out honestly; in the course of elaboration, these considerations always remain subsidiary in their status to the vision itself, no matter how much they admit of further development and refinement. The vision of philosophy's meaning and function has now been set forth in detail and I hope with commensurate precision in its articulation. My main purpose has not been to denigrate either those philosophies or those conceptions of philosophy which the utterance-theory, as espoused here, happens not to delimit, encompass, or even to endorse. I also do not share in Kierkegaard's corrosive cynicism concerning the extent to which we may or may not say that novelty and real progress exist or have been made in philosophy. Kierkegaard compares some philosophies to mathematical demonstrations, saying that they begin with the statement of a theorem and wind up just where they began, except for adding "QED." It is unclear whether he (a) fails to appreciate the arguments that take place between initial statement and the completion of proof, (b) does not avow their existence, or else (c) regards philosophies of this kind as consisting of nothing but a tissue of assertions, perhaps question-begging ones at that, whose pretended rigor amounts to nothing but noise and smoke.

In any case, SK lampoons unnamed opponents by having the narrator opine that "it was a shame they never explained things, for there might well be someone who needed explanation. J. C. understood that the speaker we are talking of[32] was only reminding his hearers of things well known, and therefore there was no need of any explanation. . . . This was characteristic. Whenever the philosophers met together they enjoyed their own wisdom, and it never occurred to them to give a little help to the

32. The corresponding section in *De Omnibus* is entitled "How does the individual stand in relation to our Sentence?" (p. 130), so presumably the speaker could be anyone.

weak."[33] It might be thought from this broadside that SK
agrees with the Wittgensteinian position (foreshadowed by
Schopenhauer) that philosophy is in a vital sense noninfor-
mational, that it only "describes," never "rearranges," and
furthermore, that what it describes is (*pace* John Wisdom)
what everyone already knows, its only distinction lying in
its employment of exotic instead of quotidian terminology;
in short, that philosophy "leaves everything" just where it
is, not out of ontological politeness but due to metaphysical
impotence. I rather think, however, that what legitimately
unnerves SK is the privacy, the secrecy, the shroud surrounding philosophy, or at least the philosophy against
which he wars—the philosophy that requires "talent" but
not "authority" to master, and that has its own peculiar initiation rites,[34] rites involving mastery of arcane but apparently pointless techniques, which are learned for their own
sake, if for anything.

Against this, Kierkegaard poses his own conception of
philosophy; a standard that is not only jargon-free but *publicly verifiable;* and verifiable not merely in principle, as
scientific hypotheses are (but which in practice require an
indoctrination into the specialties of scientific method), but
in the actual practice of individuals, both in judging themselves and observing others. On this final point I am happy
to concur with Kierkegaard, and to side with him resolutely
against the forces of more impersonal types of *theoria.*

The quintessence of this outlook we saw very early, and
the rest of this chapter was devoted to its expansion and sympathetic defense. It implies a view of philosophy, and a linguistic reform appropriate thereto, which I can recommend
exactly as I would uphold the superb paradox that "virtue is

33. *De Omnibus*, p. 132. The ellipsis occurs in the text; it is not a lacuna, but a
piece of punctuation.

34. These rites are not absent elsewhere; noticeably, they are found, as SK
posits, in every department of "science and scholarship" (see remarks, *Postscript*,
pp. 15, 135).

knowledge": that is, by pointing to its *instantiation* in a champion of it, in a paradigmatic figure such as Socrates. Socrates *is* philosophy; so, if we are to tell precious metal apart from base, or detect both true and false coinage, we must rely on Socratic (and Kierkegaardian) formulations to assist us in devising our own. We may diverge from them in particulars, just as Johannes Climacus might in all earnestness stray from the Cartesian fold while somehow remaining an awkward but true disciple of "methodic doubt." But the general drift of their thought, plus what that represents, remain impeccable, and therefore constitute the only route both safe and sensible for traversing the great distance between ourselves and what SK would surely term (personal and philosophic) "elevation."[35] Any worthwhile future theory of philosophic utterances can improve on this (as it must) only by taking its challenges and cues from the core of principles and methods already set forth here under the successful impetus provided by the combined forces of Socratic wisdom and Kierkegaardian insight.

---

35. *De Omnibus,* p. 133. In later writings this becomes "edification" and is allied with a Hegelian process of self-transcendence.

4

Kierkegaard and His Critics

T wo eminent American philosophers have recently published important papers excoriating the thought of
Søren Kierkegaard. First to appear was Blanshard's essay
"Kierkegaard on Faith," in 1968;[1] it was followed, in 1971,
by Edwards's "Kierekgaard and the 'Truth' of Christian-

1. Abbreviations used to refer to Kierkegaard's works are as follows: *CUP*
stands for *Concluding Unscientific Postscript*, trans. Swenson and Lowrie
(Princeton, N.J., Princeton University Press, 1941); *E/O* for *Either/Or*, 2 vols.,
trans. Swenson, Swenson and Lowrie, rev. Johnson (Princeton, N.J.: Princeton
University Press, 1954); *FT* for *Fear and Trembling*, trans. Lowrie (Princeton,
N.J.: Princeton University Press, 1954); *PF* for *Philosophical Fragments*, trans.
Swenson, commentary Thulstrup, rev. Hong (Princeton, N.J.: Princeton Univer-
sity Press, 1962. The reference to Brand Blanshard is to his "Kierkegaard on
Faith," *The Personalist* 49 (1968): 5-23. (Hereafter abbreviated as ·*KF* in the text
and notes.)

ity."[2] One purpose of this chapter is to reply to criticisms of SK made by both Blanshard and Edwards, and to rebut their principal objections. Another is, to show the philosophical significance and centrality of some leading themes in the "aesthetic" corpus of Kierkegaardian writings. My own interpretation of SK will emerge in the process of responding to the indictments handed down by these two scholars. The results, it is hoped, will include valuable methodological and historiographical lessons as well as philosophical ones. Since an approach to SK should always be grounded in the texts themselves, it can hardly be regarded as doctrinaire to add that saluting the permanent validity possessed by many of SK's ideas is dependent on acceptance of the legitimacy of the genre in which those ideas were conceived and executed as being distinctive, yet philosophical, in nature. My own presentation and recommendation of those ideas will not, of course, mimic or duplicate SK's in its literary form: this is only an indication of SK's *in*dependence from those who seek, as sympathetic scholars must, to understand him objectively and from afar.

I

Let it be noted at the outset that Blanshard and Edwards are hardly to be compared to Tweedledum and Tweedledee. That is, their respective criticisms of SK differ considerably from one another, both in their scope and basis. Their various reasons for offering a low estimate of the contributions made by Kierkegaard are seldom the same, and equally rarely are they similar. Nevertheless, there are certain points of overlap and contact between them, uniformly distressing ones, and they should be noted. Edwards in fact

2. Paul Edwards, "Kierkegaard and the 'Truth' of Christianity," *Philosophy* 46 (1971): 89-108. (Hereafter abbreviated as *KTC* in the text and notes.)

refers approvingly to Blanshard's essay *(KTC* 106n*), calling it "the most comprehensive and powerful critique of Kierkegaard's philosophy known to me." Immediately this brings up a second point. Both these authors approach SK as though there were a finished "philosophy" to be extracted from him, and thence to be criticized. Many distinguished scholars and commentators have warned against this sort of procedure,[3] but Blanshard and Edwards seem entirely oblivious of such cautionary measures. This is not merely due to their neglect of the range of reliable secondary literature, although that is a contributing factor. It is also due to forgetfulness of some elementary and well-known rules of sound scholarship. For example, both Blanshard and Edwards rely on the *CUP* for the overwhelming majority of their quotations and footnotes. About four fifths of Edwards's evidence is based upon *CUP*, while about two thirds of the documentation marshaled by Blanshard is taken from the same source. Blanshard rounds out his presentation with several references to *FT*, of which there is scant mention in Edwards's article *(KTC* 107 n24). Both authors occasionally quote from some other texts, but only when doing so supports or confirms opinions antecedently formulated and thanks largely to their respective exegeses of *CUP*.

There is no mystery why this should be so. A trend in and somewhat established tradition of SK scholarship deems CUP the most "philosophically" significant of his works. Whether or not this is justified, it is not founded upon any evaluation of their relative literary and intellectual merits; it is grounded instead in expediency, and the imperatives of mere taste. *CUP* is, after all, the work in which SK confesses to his employment of pseudonyms *(CUP* 551ff.). A writer basing understanding of SK strictly (or chiefly) upon

---

3. See esp. Louis Mackey, reviewing Josiah Thompson, in his "Philosophy and Poetry in Kierkegaard," *Review of Metaphysics* 23 (1969) 316-32.

CUP is therefore not immediately saddled with the burden of trying to figure out whether (and if so, to what extent) any of SK's characters represent SK's personal judgments or not. There is no, or at any rate considerably less, difficulty in imputing to SK the ideas contained in *CUP*, whereas similar attributions in a number of other cases might be very risky indeed.

Not surprisingly, both Blanshard and Edwards take the "ostrich" approach to all of this. Blanshard virtually ignores the issue of the pseudonyms altogether, while Edwards, confining discussion largely to footnotes, is intelligent enough to admit that he is not, in this matter, competent to venture any theories of his own (*KTC* 106 n6). The upshot is that both scholars are compelled to restrict themselves largely to *CUP*, if not exclusively so; naturally, this prejudices their interpretations.

A good parallel might be the attempt to give a definitive account of Plato's philosophy through the medium of only one dialogue. Even if that dialogue happened to be *Republic*, *Symposium*, *Apology*, *Phaedo*, *Parmenides*, *Theaetetus*, *Phaedrus*, *Protagoras*, or *Meno*, to cite a few, the outcome would necessarily be inadequate and gravely limited, and, in view of the availability of more (and more complete) textual evidence, would inevitably appear as forced, not to say distorted, interpretation. During the medieval period, the whole of Plato to which scholars had any access (until the heyday of Islamic learning and then, finally, in the Christian world, during the time of Aristippus, whose work as translator took place in the thirteenth century) was a small section of *Timaeus*, and that not in Cicero's but only in Chalcidius's less elegant Latin version. No one could deny that the picture of Plato that necessarily emerged from such fragmentary reconstruction was, in light of what is now known, woefully inadequate. Nonetheless it was important, in that it helped provoke the movement known as "Neoplatonism," the intellectual consequences of which, from that day to this, have been incalculably great. Throughout its various transformations, from Plotinus to Ficino (and from Ficino to modern-day "essentialism" in logic), versions of Plato*nism* have been and remain enormously influential in their own right. But it does not represent nor is it equivalent to Plato, not by any stretch of the imagination. Moreover, in light of current knowledge, Platonism fails (understandably) to give Plato the benefit of any skeptical doubt, on the epistemological and metaphysical subjects for which it has become renowned, and on Plato's own supposed beliefs, in regard thereto.

A similar caveat is quite in order for the SK interpreter. To overlook over twenty other volumes in favor of one, that is, to pursue *CUP* at the expense of so many other accessible writings, is bound to have disastrous consequences, from the standpoint of accurate, comprehensive (or, as SK might puckishly say, "approximate") characterization of his thought. Edwards does say, and Blanshard would doubtless concur, that whether SK actually held certain views matters not, but only performing a critique of those ideas, taken in themselves. This kind of philosophy-in-a-vacuum is however self-defeating, for two major reasons: first, if it is only the ideas that matter, then why bother to use SK as a foil? Might it not be convenient to dispense with sources altogether, and thereby to avoid the possibility of attacking a straw man? Second, since Kierkegaard's views are, admittedly, very influential, does this not entail that philosophers should attempt to discern exactly (or as nearly correctly as is possible) just what they were, on the provisional assumption that Kierkegaard's great influence is perhaps deserved? Both Blanshard and Edwards feel that Kierkegaard's ideas lack merit, or at least, the ideas that *they* present as being Kierkegaardian. If so, why waste time and energy in demolishing them? Why not proceed instead with the hypothesis that a study of SK might yield some unexpected benefits, as opposed to caricatures of his actual views? Such a salutary idea unfortunately never occurs either to Blanshard or Edwards, however. More's the pity.

II

Blanshard's troubles with Kierkegaard are fairly easy to sketch. He concedes great personal disappointment, brought on by the "high expectation" with which he began study of SK (*KF* 19) and not met or fulfilled by the actual encounter. Why did this happen? Primarily, because Blanshard imposed his own standards on SK, his own standards as to what constitutes philosophy (and what does not). As a result, his "disillusionment" became severe: "Kierkegaard, if a philosopher at all, is a distinct species of philosophe- r. . .it is useless to look for clearly stated theses, still less for ordered arguments" (*KF* 20) in his writings. This betrays a complete misunderstanding both of the aims and of the manner of executing them that engaged SK. One would think that Blanshard would surely realize that SK's numerous attacks on "speculation" preclude (from the standpoint of internal consistency or faithfulness) any possibility of conducting polemics in the style of philosophy to which SK opposes his own iconoclastic brand of thought. What Blanshard, as a latter-day Hegelian, really wants is for SK to "argue" and conduct himself as a Hegelian or, if not as a Hegelian, then as one of the alternatives thereto that Blanshard might yet find philosophically respectable, though not acceptable. In short, Blanshard dismisses SK because SK does not discharge intellectual obligations as Blanshard sees fit; more simply, SK fails to share Blanshard's conception of philosophy. This disagreement cuts deeper than the mere coincidence that SK's critique of "speculative" philosophy aims at Hegel as its intended target, whereas Blanshard is a modern, hence defensive, proponent of Absolute Idealism. It is a profounder difference, over objectives, intentions, legitimate preoccupations. Blanshard is simply not sensitive, not open, to SK's indictment of the in-principle limitations suffered by rational thought, and this in spite of the prevalence of that theme even in the selected pieces of evidence upon which Blanshard is forced to rest his case (see *CUP* 147, 152, 158, 160, e.g.). To ask a rhetorical question, could this blindness be due to Blanshard's own wholehearted adoption of the tenets of rational thought?

Another sign that shows Blanshard's inability to grasp SK is his insistence on drawing inept and unflattering comparisons. "What was the truth that Kierkegaard saw? The great insight claimed for him is that in religion objective thinking breaks down and that the insight it seeks is obtainable by faith. As for the inadequacy of thought, a case can certainly be made for it. . . . Kierkegaard's own case is unimpressive. His contention that thought cannot deal with existence is put so obscurely that there is difficulty in extracting from it a meaning clear enough to refute" *(KF* 20-21). According to Blanshard, an impressive case (as opposed to SK's own) for the breakdown of intellectual categories in the sphere of religious faith *was* made, by Dean Mansel. This judgment is itself worth detailed investigation.

Mansel's writings are completely forgotten today, and for good reason (although Blanshard might want to say that this, along with Kierkegaard's own ever-growing popularity, is simply a sad mistake, and can be explained only on the basis of inferring or postulating a corresponding increase in human stupidity, i.e., a rise in "irrationalism"). Mansel is known today chiefly through J. S. Mill's discussion in the *Examination of Hamilton (1865)*, where Mill explains all pertinent matters, and does so with unrelenting and scrupulous fairness. Now, Mansel received the impetus for some of his own ideas from a consideration of the problem of evil. This perennial dilemma could be settled, or so he thought, by relying upon the inscrutability of God, that is, incomparability between God, as infinite being, and the rest of creation, and, armed with that, point out the resultant incommensurability and (to man) incomprehensibility of the Supreme Being. This is an old, albeit an ignoble, gambit. I say this because the distinguished line of theologians who first appealed to it (pseudo-Dionysius, Scotus Erigena, Anselm, and to some extent Aquinas) were bent on overcoming theoretical obstacles standing in the way of their own intellectual formulations, and eventually were compelled to claim to have much more rational and cognitional insight into Godhead than such strategy would ever license them to invoke. For example, Aquinas draws a distinction between propositions that are "self-evident in themselves" and those which are "self-evident to us" (*Summa Contra Gentiles*, 1. 10-13; *Summa Theologiae*, 1a. 2. 1), treating the ontological argument. This enables him to claim that we can know *that* God exists, but little or nothing about *what* He is; it also enables him to suggest that God's existence, while a necessary truth, is not one that we can deduce—it is a case of (permanently) concealed analyticity. Hence our knowledge or discovery of God can be neither mystical nor, in a strict sense, rational: instead, it must be *in*ductive and empirical. The elaboration of the Five Ways (*S.T.* 1a. 2,3) is thereby accounted for; but in this explanation, what the expositor sympathetic to St. Thomas must try to overlook is the way in which exploration of nature to find the "effects" of God's handiwork can lead only to definite conclusions provided that we already possess (or else can infer) a definite conception of God as the cause of the phenomena observed and investigated: and this antecedent, definite, and derived conception of God (as omnipotent, omniscient, benevolent, and, in Aquinas's case, as "unlimited *esse*" or act of being; *S.T.* 1a. 3.4), commits one to making a claim to far more (human) knowledge of God than had, initially, been bargained for. Likewise with Mansel; for while man is not thought capable of reaching truths about God, yet the explanation for the existence of worldly evil is predicated on the assumption that God makes, as a matter of course, certain adjustments in the balance or preponderance of good over evil in the world (which idea recalls St. Augustine's shop-worn "tapestry" sophism). This means that whatever Mansel offers, he too must claim to know more about how God operates than any pious outbursts of theological modesty might originally indicate.

Mill's own rebuttal of Mansel is not even directed at these shortcomings, however. (Oddly, Blanshard criticizes Kierkegaard for failing to adjust and clarify his "theory of knowledge" *(KF* 21), when the fact is that SK has *no* theory of knowledge, not even tacitly or by implication, and contrary to what Blanshard's inspection suggests. Apparently, neither did Mansel, or else Mill would undoubtedly have been quick to expound it. Here again, Blanshard's lack of subtlety, criticizing SK on non-SK terms, is sadly evident). Mill instead remarks, with robust pre-Rylean linguistic spirit, that the use of such terms as "good" and "evil" as applied to Divine characteristics is and must be parasitic upon their original, homelier application to human moral contexts. Consequently, Mill argues, if a term such as "evil" cannot in principle be used to describe actions of God in a manner similar to its understood use for the characterization of human action (and personality), then it cannot be intelligibly applied at all. Correlatively, the same logic would hold for the expression "good." Consequently, as Mill correctly insists, it is not possible to exonerate God from the problem of evil merely by claiming a drastic shift in the meaning of the word, from its human to its God-referring employment. There must be some uniformity in its meaning; theological must (logically as well as genetically) be posterior to mundane contexts, in order that it qualify as intelligible, expressible, communicable.

This is of course tantamount to a rejection of both Neoplatonist metaphysics and Thomistic analogy-theory. In a way, this is nothing if not an elaborate restatement of that famous chestnut stemming from Plato's *Euthyphro (10A)*, concerning whether the gods love what is pious *(to hosios)* because it is pious, or whether it is pious because they love it. If the latter, then the denotation as well as the meaning of "piety" depends upon an arbitrary (voluntarist) whim and caprice, and, as Plato is quick to remark, the Greek gods are not reliable as moral authorities, in light of their own record of behavior. If the former, then the gods' love of piety is (a) tautologous, since by definition they would not be godlike, or gods, if they did not; (b) correspondingly uninformative, since it tells us nothing about the nature of piety. The moral usually drawn from this is that religion, that is, the introduction of religious concepts, is logically irrelevant to morality—it contributes nothing toward the justification of fundamental moral notions. So much, then, for the justly forgotten Mansel! As for SK—note that Kierkegaard, himself a dedicated Plato scholar (witness *The Concept of Irony)*, actually welcomes such a challenge, inasmuch as he likewise feels that religious and moral categories do not mix, and are logically independent of one another.

This is at least one outstanding ramification of SK's famous "teleological suspension of the ethical," of which Blanshard is almost blissfully unaware. At this point it is therefore both necessary and desirable to consider the teleological suspension in its own right. It is entirely misconstrued if seen as representing a conflict of duties,[4] which mistake does happen, often enough, in SK literature. The reason for this error lies not with SK's own use of the story of Abraham and Isaac (see *FT* 26-29) so much as owing to perplexities occasioned by the story itself (for which see

4. For by far the best version of this still-mistaken reading, see John Donnelly, "Søren Kierkegaard's 'Teleological Suspension of the Ethical': A Reinterpretation," Ph. D. diss., Brown University, 1970. A published segment of this thesis appears as "Re-examining Søren Kierkegaard's 'Teleological Suspension of the Ethical,' " in John Donnelly, ed., *Logical Analysis and Contemporary Theism* (New York: Fordham University Press, 1972), pp. 294-331.

There is an interesting discussion of a related problem in James Rachels, "God and Human Attitudes," *Religious Studies* 7 (1971): 325-37 (and Robert A. Oakes, "Reply to Prof. Rachels," *ibid.* 8 (1972): 165-67). Rachels attempts, in the Findlay tradition, to *dis*prove the existence of God. His endeavor is not based on logical or epistemic grounds, but on the premise that if God were a being fit to be worshipped (which for Rachels is equivalent to being worthy of unconditional obedience), then it should follow that human moral autonomy is destroyed. This consequence is taken as (a) undesirable, from God's standpoint and therefore as (b) indicating an incoherency in the concept of God, at least insofar as the Divine relates ethically to the human. However, Rachels ignores several things: 1. the Fall, which "proves" that "willful disobedience" is possible, even from within the theistic framework; 2. the fact that "worship" neither entails nor is synonymous with "unconditional obedience" (nor would the converse relationship, whether it be one of identity or established by inference, obtain); 3. that adherence to the commands of God is quite freely chosen, as, for example, in Abraham's case, or else the examination of his knighthood of faith would be superfluous, hence question begging. Therefore the moral freedom or independence enjoyed by human agents is neither lost nor tampered with, not *pace* SK, at least.

However, Rachels does (obliquely) raise another issue: given God's *foreknowledge*, is not the ordeal that Abraham and Isaac endured totally unnecessary? If so, that is, if God knows the outcome of the trial in advance, is He not merciless in making them go through with the three-day journey, to the very brink of committing the "murder"? Is it not cruel for God to make them undergo these tortures, to the brink of execution? But it is not the act that counts, for SK, but rather the spirit or intention in which it is undertaken (see George Schrader, "Kant and Kierkegaard on Duty and Inclination," *Journal of Philosophy*, 65 (1968): 688-701). If God is cruel, then, this tells something about God, relative to Rachel's premise: namely, that he is *not* worthy of worship, let alone of unquestioned obedience. This result may even support the suggested reading of SK as an antireligious parodist in spite of himself; if not, it at least indicates where and when the parting of conceptual (ethical *vs.* religious) ways must come. It also argues in favor of the "incomprehensibility" thesis, and hence the (classical) interpretations of "paradox" and "absurdity." On this topic in *CUP*, see further Herbert M. Garelick, *The Anti-Christianity of Kierkegaard* (The Hague and New York: Martinus Nijhoff, 1965-66); cited by Edwards, *KTC* 107 n23.

Genesis 22:1-19). Why does Abraham withhold truth from
Isaac, that is, information about the (apparent) purpose of
their journey to Mt. Moriah? Presumably because he might
have a difficult time persuading Isaac to accompany him!
Kierkegaard anticipates this psychological hurdle, in that (in
FT) he imagines Abraham as deceiving Isaac, solely in
order that the son not "lose faith" in God: for, better that
Isaac should be shocked by his father's actions, and blame
the episode on Abraham, than transfer assessment of blame
onto God. (Therein lurks a thinly veiled allusion to SK's
wayward personal relationship with Regina Olsen; for Blanshard's keen yet derogatory discussion of this affair, see *KF*,
16-17).[5]

But *why* should Isaac lose faith in God, in the first place?
And why should Abraham even be concerned lest this happen? Put another way, if Isaac *were* to lose his faith, as a
result of being told that God had commanded Abraham to
sacrifice his dearest relation and only son, would that not
be *justifiable* loss of faith? In short, is not Abraham, in un-
supportably keeping the truth from Isaac, shielding his son
from the opportunity to draw unedifying yet impeccably
logical consequences about God, deductions that Abraham,
for reasons known only to himself, does not wish to see dis-
closed? Laconically, Abraham says "God himself will supply
the burnt offering." Isaac implicitly trusts Abraham in precisely the manner in which Abraham in turn trusts in God
the Father. But, is such trust no longer *merited?*

5. I find myself in reluctant agreement with Blanshard's assessment of SK's
"too celebrated love affair" (*KF* 17), and his restrained conclusions that (1) "as
Buber suggested, God was Regina's successful rival" (*KF* 18); (2) "by merely secular standards, his behavior was that of a cad" (*KF* 18). The reader should judge for
himself whether Blanshard is also right in unreservedly calling SK "mentally and
sexually abnormal. . .a mind in which a messianic egoism was mixed in unwhole-
some fashion with eroticism and piety" (*KF* 18), or about his characterization of
SK as a "strange blend of piety and contempt. . ." (*KF* 20), which portrayal Blanshard attributes to Brandes. Blanshard is aware that he is resorting to an *ad
hominem* onslaught (*KF* 16), but he also recognizes that in Kierkegaard's case, it
somehow seems unavoidable, or at least fascinatingly irresistible.

Raising this issue brings forth a related one. Perhaps Abraham (secretly) realizes or suspects that everything will work out for the best, in the end. He could arrive at this startling conclusion through several different routes and processes: by entertaining an encompassing, naive, facile, and shallow optimism (admittedly, most unlikely); by a reasoning-out that determines that it would be contradictory, and hence is impossible, for God to command one to do the forbidden; or by reliance on the earlier word of God, namely, the solemn promise (recounted in Genesis 12) to continue Abraham's seed on through descendants. Leaving the first possibility aside, the latter two both involve what Kierkegaard certainly must have considered "fudging" on the main point, that is, an evasion of the trial, the trial to be endured by every aspiring (or every called) knight of faith. Specifically, the middle alternative stumbles over what SK calls "temptation," in the sense of the drive or urge to think, to reason, to invoke certain intellectual categories. The last possibility has an obvious self-interest rationale, and therefore is also in diametric opposition to the Kierkegaardian demand for blind faith, as a test of religiosity in crisis situations. Hence such ways of overcoming the "teleological suspension of the ethical" as have just been cited do not surmount it at all, but abjectly fail the first test that partly qualifies one for transcendent knighthood.

Kierkegaard's own solution, of course, is heavily imbued with the affective criterion of inwardness; it bids Abraham to be silent, asks him deliberately to conceal his motives, and to suffer the pain of whatever worldly consequences may arise therefrom, without ever trying to defend himself against personal criticism, or even punishment. Abraham must incur the risk of appearing to the world, to the public, as a cheat, as a sneaky fellow, as a lunatic if need be, and must bear all this in unresentful, guileless silence. He must protect his own as well as God's "incognito," to signify his disdain for and preparedness to relinquish everything this-worldly. The God-relationship must be kept privileged, which means private, or strictly personal.

This concurs with SK's separation of the religious sphere from that of secular life, with the latter's concern for personal autonomy, obedience to impersonal (universal, law-like) imperatives, and this-worldly—or interpersonal—self-sufficiency. The man of religiousness B (Abraham, as a heroic knight of faith, goes *beyond* the requirements neces-sary to reach this stage, but exactly in so doing, incorpo-rates or embodies its salient traits) is one who has pros-trated himself before a personal, or better to say, supraper-sonal authority, has accepted His Word as binding upon himself, and is prepared to break or supersede allegiance to all mundane pursuits, norms, and obligations. This convic-tion is cemented through a process of "self-annihilation," which is at first unable to conceive of divinity except in the traditional, conceptual terms of atemporal, nonspatial ex-istence; ensuing guilt at the thought of the ontological dis-parity between man and God provides a temporary emo-tional resting place, labeled religiousness A. From it, the individual *may* move to B, and adopt a personal God as his Savior (Jesus Christ, for instance), or he may "backslide" (a term of my own coinage) into the stage of ethicality; unable to relate himself to the paradox and mystery of a transcen-dent divinity made human (incarnate), of God become man, and for the express purpose, *not* of providing for human re-demption, but of enduring suffering for suffering's sake (*CUP* 433, 530). "A" is a volatile and unpredictable affective location; that is, no man remains in it for very long, but, where he goes after being in it cannot be rationally deter-mined with any confidence, since it concerns the most in-ward states of feeling and (unobservable) despair. "B" is cumulative, that is, depends on "A" as a precedent stage, but is *not* related to "A" as effect to cause.

III

These conceptions serve to illustrate not only the sharp differences between SK and Mansel, but the ignorance in which Blanshard conducts his polemic. It remains to consider his attack on the integrity of *FT*:

> What are we to say of a rhapsody. . .in praise of pure and holy murder, of a defense of the humanly immoral on the ground that it is religious duty? Kierkegaard, in choosing such ground, . . .has cut off the possibility of rational criticism. . .an appeal. . .to the unintelligible and irrational. . .is begging the question. *(KF 10)*

Blanshard goes on to observe, correctly, that claim to "divine warrant" cannot be criticized rationally, but can only bring forth denunciations from each side. Blanshard's own accusation is simply that SK is a "moral nihilist," in virtue of his readiness, not so much to condone murder, as to "deliberately" abandon sense and reason. In this way Blanshard expressly states his dubiousness over the merits of "the second half of the great insight attributed to [SK]. . .that where reason fails faith succeeds" *(KF 21)*. What can be said about it?

Blanshard certainly puts a finger on the nerve of Kierkegaardian thought. But precisely what has Blanshard discovered? That SK is a precursor of Barth? That "belief cannot argue with unbelief, but only preach to it"? Possibly. But what he omits mention of is that Kierkegaard is *as* puzzled by Abraham as Blanshard professes himself to be: "Abraham I cannot understand, I can only admire him" *(FT* 121). For how can one admire a person he cannot understand? Does not admiration have to go beyond, in the sense of presupposing, understanding? The dilemma concealed here is the commitment to "belief in the paradox," of late a source of major confusion in SK scholarship (commented on by Edwards, *KTC* 107, n23). This problem, like its near relation "the absurd," cannot be given a settled interpretation in a few lines or paragraphs. Suffice it to remark that Blanshard shows no awareness of two prominent exegetical items, items that form parts of a unified position, thereby generating a perspective quite fruitful for SK research. And these are as follows:

(a) SK's controlling question is *not* "What is it to be a man?" or "How can I become a Christian?"[6] These are important, but subsidiary. The main question is, what does it *mean* to be a Christian? The emphasis is therefore universal, that is, falls squarely on the individual reader, rather than on the author (in which latter case it would become therapeutic, self-therapeutic in fact,[7] and therefore of questionable value or utility in its formalized version, i.e., as literature). Speaking broadly, the dominant concern is with the *psychological* requirements and demands that are placed upon the agent, or would-be believer: in short, *what does it mean to be religious?* (Since SK at times identifies religiousness B with Christianity, his own platform is narrower in scope than the universal message that can legitimately be extracted from reading his works). Nowhere in the "aesthetic" corpus does SK either endorse or condemn projected fulfillment of those criteria explicitly, although his biographically overt, philosophically covert attitudes are indirectly accessible.

(b) Inasmuch as SK is frequently revered for his greatness as an ironist, it is entirely possible, and indeed plausible, that his "aesthetic" works may be read as implicit *satire* upon religion/Christianity: not in the style of Voltairean ridicule, nor in the manner of Shavian farce, but indictment

6. See Louis Mackey, *Kierkegaard: A Kind of Poet* (Philadelphia: Pennsylvania University Press, 1971), p. 133. Also John Passmore, *A Hundred Years of Philosophy*, rev. ed. (Baltimore, Md.: Penguin Books, 1968), p. 468.
7. For this approach to SK, see Josiah Thompson, *The Lonely Labyrinth: Kierkegaard's Pseudonymous Works* (Carbondale, Ill: Southern Illinois University Press, 1967).

of the very conditions, criteria, and requirements announced under heading (a). The consequences of examining this interpretation have not been sufficiently developed, indeed have never been dwelt upon anywhere, at any length. They should be considered, if only in light of Climacus's strange and singular declaration, apparently one made for reasons besides the obvious token of modesty, that he is emphatically not a Christian (*CUP* 457, 488, 528, 545). This can hardly be entirely unintentional self-revelation, or self-revelation merely. Blanshard ignores all this; hence his indisposed, needlessly hostile, and unappreciative essay pursues an ultra-literal, predetermined course. My own approach may at first seem born of extreme exegetical despair. However, as we now turn to scrutinize Edwards, it may strike us as having considerably more to offer, in the way of a sound methodology for understanding SK, than either Blanshard or Edwards has at his command and disposal.

IV

Edwards's attack on Kierkegaard is relatively sophisticated. Unlike Blanshard, Edwards does not have an axe to grind, at least, not an obtrusive one! However, he is in accord with Blanshard, not only in his low estimation of SK, but in the general tenor of his article: both scholars feel themselves called upon to attack and denigrate SK as the representative of a tradition (existentialism) with which they disagree. This alone shows that their reading of SK has been conducted "in bad faith," or, to use an untechnical but coined expression, with prejudice "aforeunthought". Kierkegaard is notorious for denying the "ethical reality" of all save the given individual. But Blanshard and Edwards tend never to see or to read SK as an individual author, but instead view him as a partisan, as a spokesman on behalf of a school or tradition (which they understand only very imperfectly)—a tradition that SK inaugurated, albeit by way of Brandes, Nietzsche, and various delayed literary reactions thereto. So Edwards, like Blanshard, filters his judgment of SK through a number of very poorly focused lenses. If Edwards knew—that is, were prepared to acknowledge—more about SK, he could not imaginably arrive at half of the negative conclusions that lack of preparation for the special rigors of dealing with Kierkegaard compels him to reach.

Nonetheless, Edwards is sensitive to some points. He contends, to cite one example, that the use of the word *true* in the controversial context of "subjectivity is truth" constitutes an uninformative muddle *(KTC* 101-2), but he steadfastly refuses to give SK the slightest benefit of any doubt: of allowing for the limitations of SK's philosophical vocabulary, in contrast with the sophistication of modern-day language analysis. As a result, Edwards consistently misses the point about "edification" *(cf. E/O* 2:356), one that SK is ever prone to make. Since Edwards is anyway not primarily concerned with exploring "inwardness" or "passionate appropriation," this omission is, for him, hardly surprising. (To make up the deficiency, one should certainly read Louis Mackey's brilliant book,[8] there being no shortcuts to deep and whole understanding of SK in this area).

Edwards's main concern instead lies with the existence of God *(KTC* 98) and SK's polemics thereon. Throughout, Edwards's cardinal mistake is to *assume* that SK is bent on defending religious (or at any rate, theistic) orthodoxy. In view of the recommendation stated in (b), above, this procedure is very wrong-headed. I shall suggest how and why, momentarily.

8. Louis Mackey, *Kierkegaard: A Kind of Poet* (Philadelphia: Pennsylvania University Press, 1971), esp. chaps. 2,3, and 6.

Edwards's major conclusion is that SK's postures are each and all ". . .consistent with the most thorough-going atheism" *(KTC* 99). The question is rather whether SK's (deliberate?) position in the *Postscript,* insofar as one can be gleaned from the verbose outpourings of the philosophical protagonist, Johannes, does or does not *entail* an atheism of sorts. This goes considerably beyond Edwards in boldness, yet need not do SK any injustice. Even if this conjecture is rejected, at least this much can be said in attempting to summarize the obscure teaching of *CUP;* namely, that in principle no person can *understand* religious belief, the actual ways of the believer, from outside, or without sharing or participating in that belief. (And belief, being intensely private and personal, cannot be shared in at all, at least not in the manner in which communities, groups, or families share in responsibilities or in the distribution of goods.) Abraham's behavior, as described in lyric and rhapsodic terms in *FT,* lends credence to this hypothesis even while illustrating it; on the plane of ethico-religious immanence, not yet transcended by ties to personal authority, the professions if not the actual practice of Judge Wilhelm in *E/O* are another manifestation and documentation of it. SK makes this implication clear in a number of places *(FT* 49; *CUP* 370, 424, 450n, 515).[9] Consequently, given the perspective of the neutral or detached observer—the scientist or scholar—religious forms of conduct, no matter what their content, will, quite unavoidably, appear uniformly erratic and bizarre, if they are genuinely religious in the SK-ian sense. That this skewing of appearances should occur is quite natural, in virtue of the following considerations: (i) likely condemnation of such phenomena as alike being indications of fanaticism, thereby signifying that "detachment"

9. For good discussion, see Louis Mackey, "The Poetry of Inwardness," repr. in Josiah Thompson, ed., *Kierkegaard: A Collection of Critical Essays* (Garden City, N.Y.: Doubleday, 1972), esp. p. 53.

is really symptomatic of an entrenched and rival position (e.g., Humean skepticism, of which a healthy dose is injected in both Edwards and Blanshard); (ii) systematically passing over SK's own denunciations of fanaticism, fanaticism being construed as the attempt to impose deeply felt or held views on others, presumptuously to set others' beliefs in order prior to arriving at, arranging, and caring for beliefs of one's own—the latter being a lifelong task in itself (see esp. *CUP* 29, also 32, 534; 166, 26f, 327, 520, 523, 535, 537 and 538): (iii) inability of the observer to assess religious feeling and belief, not owing to any particular irreligiosity, but because, according to SK, such objective spectators are not truly "existing individuals." Correspondingly, they cannot comprehend the progression of existence- "stages" at all; neither the experience of the individual *étapes*, nor the inner upheavals causing *Aufhebung* from one to another in those persons so constituted as to undergo this form of spiritual transcendence can be grasped.

What this means for the SK scholar is, in its plainest terms, that something like an intangible correlate of the familiar historical method of "empathy" is necessary in order for intelligent criticism of SK to be possible. A work's intelligibility is not conferred upon the reader by anything short of that. Of course, this kind of identification cannot be merely provisional or an "act," lest it degenerate into sham. It must take the form of personal commitment, prepared for in advance by way of a wholesale, sympathetic immersion in heretofore alien and unappreciated outlooks. Even anthropologists are trained for (routine) capability to exhibit such tolerance. It follows, then, that neither Blanshard nor Edwards is suited to the task of reading, much less of criticizing, SK.[10]

10. Compare the insightful remark of Mackey: "The reader who is already committed to a given view of life will revel in its presentation by the Kierkegaar-

V

When we turn to Edwards's supposedly most devastating argument, we can best see what it inadvertently exposes. He writes:

Let us suppose that Kierkegaard was mistaken about the nature of God and that what God prizes is intellectual rectitude and not the feverish inwardness that Kierkegaard valued so highly. Let us suppose that when Kierkegaard comes up for judgment God addresses him with these words: "You led a miserable and contemptible life. The last man I judged was a Scottish philosopher by the name of David Hume and I rewarded him with eternal bliss. He did not believe in immortality, he did not beleive in my existence, and he most emphatically rejected the doctrine of the incarnation. He was right on the last point—for your information Jesus was just a man, in many ways an admirable man, but he was not my son. Hume's unbelief in immortality and my existence were errors but they were most creditable errors since he followed the best available evidence, which is all that a human being can do. He followed the available evidence although it took great courage to do so since the conclusions were anything but pleasant. You on the other hand were a coward. You refused to follow the evidence and concocted all sorts of crudely fallacious theories to make yourself believe the pleasant conclusion that you would live happily forever. I detest such cowardice. Because of my merciful constitution I will not sentence you to eternal damnation but will extinguish you anon." (*KTC* 97-98)

Edwards goes on to predict, as it were, that if SK were to be confronted by such a God, he would not consider him-

dian pseudonym. He who is not committed may well become sick of it and throw it all up." I do not share Mackey's facile optimism when he goes on, however, to conjecture that "whether he like it or lump it, he will have got the message. . . ." (*Kierkegaard: A Kind of Poet*, p. 322 n27). I am afraid this does not apply to the two scholars here in question, at any rate.

self "vindicated" nor remain unrepentant, but would instead see himself as "defeated and refuted" on his own terms—that is, in the prospects of his own salvation (*KTC* 90, in *re CUP* 20).

What can be said in answer to this swift succession of charges? The following replies could well be in order:

What makes Edwards suppose that God's judgments are carried out in the manner that Edwards finds pleasing? How can Edwards, any more than SK (or Aquinas), claim to comprehend the ways of God, or to possess insight into God's thinking, concerning something as important and decisive as human salvation? (And this holds, even allowing for Edwards's professed atheism, for in that case, his discussion of God is an avowedly fictional representation.) And Kierkegaard could add that the situation that Edwards pictures may even violate the conditions that define God's gratuitous interest in (being loved by) creation; therefore it simply never can arise. Edwards's God-conception is not only fanciful but wrong; borrowing the strong, although entirely misdirected, language of Blanshard (*KF* 10), it is an "impostor" masquerading as divinity. The purpose of the masquerade is argumentative, but the argument is self-defeating and therefore cannot be carried to its desired end.

Hume may have followed the best available evidence, but evidently (if the story is to be believed) that evidence was not good enough. Being open, undogmatic, and "rational" in a broad sense are not acceptable substitutes for being right, especially in something as important as God's existence!

Moreover, did Hume merely "follow" evidence, or did he actually invent and supply the preponderance of that which favored his own skeptical views? Did he, in the *Dialogues* as well as in the *Natural History of Religion*, both of which are works that Kierkegaard was familiar with, simply copy the reasonings of certain predecessors, or did he not rather work out, meticulously and with great originality, a penetrating logic of validation, based entirely on his own intellectual resources? Also, if this logic is unmistakably hostile to stated religious interests, why was it so well received by such diverse (yet equally reactionary, i.e., fideist) thinkers as Hamann and Schleiermacher, respectively? Why was it found so intriguing for its religious possibilities, in clarifying the grounds of and for faith, if its intent was so unambiguously threatening to religious causes?

And, why would the elements of Humean methodology be inimical to religion if they were acknowledged (by him) to be derived from the stock of analytical concepts propounded by the most pious members of the Port-Royal Jansenists of the seventeenth century?

Is "evidence" the manner in which God's existence is decided? Not according to many of the received traditions of theology, both classical and as located in the Kierkegaard of the *Fragments* (see *PF* 46, 92). For just as logical proofs are for SK a sign of loss, lack, or cosmeticized disappearance of faith (*CUP* 31, 485), so too he never tires of saying that Christianity is not "an historical event" at all: "It is subjectivity that Christianity is concerned with, and it is only in subjectivity that its truth exists, if it exists at all; objectively, Christianity has absolutely no existence" (*CUP* 116). And recall that ". . .no one ever becomes devout objectively" (*CUP* 118). Edwards's imported ground rules preclude SK even from setting up conditions for faith, while SK's (see esp. *CUP* 23, 109) should preclude Edwards from making any of his accusations stick. Blanshard in effect comments on this cross-purposive state of affairs, and very nicely: "If. . .irrational faith is accepted, the principles on which reflection conducts itself are everywhere inpugned. . . . Kierkegaard should merely smile like Buddha and remain silent" (*KF* 15). Indeed, so must Edwards!

Otherwise, denigration of SK will only resemble SK's admiration for Abraham, in being that which *by-passes* understanding.

What leads Edwards to assert that Christ is not God's son? Is this not arrant theological (or presumptively antitheological) dogmatism on his part? (My scholarly preoccupation, from the vantage point of historico-philosophic accuracy, lies chiefly in preserving Christological doctrines intact; let cries of outrage be confined to the needless excitation of murmurs among adversaries and, as Hume would say, the zealots.) My suspicion is, that Edwards is puckishly attempting to duplicate or mimic what he (quite wrongly) takes to be SK-ian authoritarianism.

Biographical knowledge makes it clear that Hume never found living with the heretical conclusions he defended to be uncomfortable or unpleasant. His only expressed self-doubt concerned the viability of his theory of the self (*Treatise*, 1. 4. 6-7 and Appendix, following Bk. 3), which is a consequence of the failure of his epistemological atomism to deal adequately with questions of personal identity. Hume's *Inquiry Concerning The Principles of Morals* sheds much light on his view of human destiny, and shows that human life can be gratifying, once the ghastly institutional encumbrances of priestly morality and its accompanying train of "monkish virtues" are eliminated.[11] In this respect, Hume remained an unreconstructed child of the Englightenment: like Voltaire, his goal was to rub out the "infamy" of both the Church and corrupt State, in favor of the untrammeled enjoyment and wholesome self-assertion of the spontaneous, healthy individual in mutual partnership

11. See David Hume, *An Inuqiry Concerning the Principles of Morals,* ed. C. W. Hendel (Indianapolis, Ind.: Bobbs-Merrill, 1957), pp. 89, 91, 93, 98, 141, 158. On Hume's ridicule of transubstantiation, see *A Treatise of Human Nature,* ed. L. H. Selby-Bigge (Oxford: Clarendon Press, 1888), p. 524. Some scholars, notably R. H. Popkin, have argued for the influence of Hume on SK. I do not accept this contention, but I do perceive the occasional slight resemblances between them.

with his human peers. Against this ideal, SK's may seem overly morbid; but there is at least (curiously enough) this intellectual lacuna in the *Postscript:* namely, no discussion, and only the barest elliptical mention, of the notion of Hell *(CUP* 20, 87)! Had Edwards focused on this aspect of SK's thought, or attempted to ponder the omission of any consideration of the implications of (divine or personally inflicted) eternal punishment, he might well have made his criticisms forceful ones. As it is, the major points of vulnerability are left unnoticed, and the profundity of SK's *lapses* goes as unrecognized as his signal intellectual and moral achievements. The best one can say is that Edwards's attack is, as it stands, grossly incomplete, as well as far off-target.

VI

Nevertheless, it would be wrong to say that Edwards never succeeds in spotting glaring weaknesses in the structure of SK-ian thought. We must now consider these, and then we shall be able to see whether an effective response can be devised.[12] To quote Edwards once more:

> To say that only a believer can attain the highest form of existence is not at all the same thing as to say that what the believer believes is true. *(KTC* 99)

Mackey might have us counter that Kierkegaard is a "poet" and therefore that undue concern with truth-values is misplaced, indeed the sign of a methodological category mistake. Edwards could always retort that, at the risk of promulgating textual distortion, it is only "religious propositions"

---

12. I have discussed this at length in my review of Mackey's *Kierkegaard: A Kind of Poet,* in *Kierkegaardiana* (1974): 76-82.

that he is justifiably interested in somehow extrapolating; never mind in case this means using SK as a foil at best, or leads to presenting a caricature of SK at worst *(KTC* 106 n6). I am therefore inclined, for once, to indulge Edwards's orientation here. Letting him continue, then:

> one important feature of Kierkegaard's position. . .[is that] Kierkegaard implies that he can tell who is worshipping the true God and who is merely worshipping an idol. The question that immediately arises. . .is whether such a discrimination is possible on Kierkegaard's principles.[13] *(KTC* 103)

Edwards goes on to say, quite creditably, that if the test for adequacy/veracity of belief is that one hold it "sincerely and without reservations," then "even the sincere and committed atheist" *(KTC* 103), whom Edwards *presumes* SK wants to exclude, would, perforce, count as a man of genuine faith. (Compare Blanshard's envisioned proliferations of Christianity, at *KF* 16). But, as Edwards adds, "there is little doubt that Kierkegaard had some awareness of this difficulty and tried to meet it" *(KTC* 103). Edwards is referring primarily to SK's distinction between immanent and transcendent religiousness (A and B), through which the difference between Christian faith and faith approximators or faith-surrogates becomes tangible. Kierkegaard adheres, I think, to the following quasi-causal thesis: that only a suitable range of stimuli is capable of provoking the appropriate psychological sentiment as-

13. A similar point is urged by Popkin, in his essay on "Kierkegaard and Scepticism," repr. in Josiah Thompson, ed., *Kierkegaard: A Collection of Critical Essays,* esp. pp. 371-72. Popkin's more reserved critique nevertheless discerns an inexpungeable element of "anarchy" pertaining to religiousness B, i.e., to the supposedly unique ways in which it is individually met, confirmed, reached, or fulfilled. Edwards judges SK's position as being filled with "chaotic implications" *(KTC* 103), in a quite similar vein. Here if anywhere Blanshard's discussion of SK's "epistemology" (or rather the disturbing lack of one) could shed some light on the grounds for unifying one's experience in one way rather than another.

sociated with the corresponding qualities deemed exemplary of religiousness B (even where this sentiment is purely internal [i.e., nonbehavioral] and therefore can in principle only be known by the individual concerned, although his own awareness of his inner condition need not ever be verbally formulated, or even formulable). Edwards acknowledges as much when he avers that ". . .because of the paradoxical nature of what is affirmed, Christianity and Christianity alone intensifies the believer's passion to its 'highest pitch.' "[14] *(KTC 104)*

At this point I am compelled to issue my own rejoinder, not so much to Edwards[15] as to SK himself. First, making

14. In transcending religiousness A, SK thinks that in religiousness B he has also alighted upon what is willingly termed the "specifically Christian religiousness" *(CUP* 493). In this regard, the key passage is at *CUP* 539: ". . .the appropriation by which a Christian is a Christian must be so specific that it cannot be confused with anything else." (Edwards's cause would be infinitely bettered were he able to quote this passage; other vexed textual points include *CUP* 497-98, 369; cf. *CUP* 181, 382).

15. Edwards asks, semi-rhetorically, ". . .can a human being really believe something that he acknowledges to be absurd?" *(KTC* 105). This is a fair question, in view of SK's predilection for delineating the psychological requirements for religiousness B. But Edwards fails, because of his own semantic preoccupation with "truth" and "subjectivity" *(KTC* 101-2), to appreciate SK's concern, concern that is not misplaced in itself, but rather in light of the compelling recognition that Kierkegaard's context is a *special* one; just as the famous concluding slogan about "edification" *(E/O* 2: 356) applies only under special circumstances, and within a restricted domain, namely, that of the "existential spheres" or stages.

Although Edwards is a far more sensitive interpreter than Blanshard, he, too, is guilty of elementary mistakes and of overly fussy, literalist scholarship. He attempts, for instance, to rescue SK from "absurdity" by latching onto the expression "improbable," which SK *does* use *(CUP* 208-9), but only as an *obvious* substitute (synonym) for "contradiction" or "paradox." There Kierkegaard writes: "The probable. . .is so little to the taste of a believer that he fears it most of all, since he well knows that when he clings to probabilities it is because he is beginning to lose his faith." From this one easily gathers what SK would say about, e.g., the famous Pascalian wager. However, this makes no impression on Edwards, who writes woodenly: ". . .if the paradox consists of statements which the believer knows to be self-contradictory, 'believing the absurd' becomes an unintelligible expression" *(KTC* 108, n 61). Precisely! And for SK this is true too, unless one considers him to be eschewing the very notion of "statement" (in favor of "existential communication"), but even in that case the expression of such communication will fall into the range of traditional logico-grammatical patterns, if only by default.

the claim that only such-and-such phenomena can actually generate the affective responses that are connected with or directly labeled as "religiousness B," is clearly to make an *empirical* claim. It is therefore neither a necessary truth (which notion SK construes as a piece of Hegelian twaddle, in any case), nor is it an unfalsifiable, performative, self-certifying proposition or utterance. It is factual, not oracular; in content, in style, it is simply a declaration about a state of affairs. As such, it is highly dubious: it is very likely empirically false, taken as an exclusivity-claim about the psychological powers of Christianity, in relation to the awakening of a "religiousness B" consciousness.

Consider too those elastic but nonvague criteria of religious belief that judicial bodies such as the United States Supreme Court are called upon from time to time to exposit. They are instructive, in that there is entertained the

One might also invoke the saying of Tertullian; but that would only show to what great extent SD has captured the *meaning* of Christianity, and does not necessarily take the further step of claiming an endorsement thereof on SK's part. Blanshard therefore is quite right when he opines that SK "as a philosophe-r. . .employed with scornful confidence the reason which, as a theologian, he dismissed with equal scorn. . .when one has bid good-bye to reason and made the prodigious non-rational leap into the rarefied air of paradox, one should presumably say nothing, since anything one did say would have to be said in the distorting accents of the reason one has left behind" (*KF*, 21). Again, exactly! Does the fact that SK keeps on talking and talking (*KF* 19-20) point up an *inconsistency* on his part, or does it instead bring out an *ironic* and negative logical commentary on all of the foregoing Kierkegaardian creeds and formulations, as carried out by SK himself? This alternative is something that Blanshard and Edwards never consider, because they do not stop to think that perhaps SK is partly on their side, or at all events not hostile to the (prematurely anti-SK) entrenched philosophical-scientific "commitments" (not specifically Idealism and logical empiricism, respectively) expressed in general, publicly shared standards for claim-testing, of reasoning, marshaling of evidence, and including respect for documentation (see *CUP* 34, 118). This possibility of alliance they cannot imagine. The worst kind of reading of, and consequently of writing about, SK is that which so frequently makes up its mind *a priori* as to what it shall discover or ignore in his works: making for an inadvertent justification for following the Biblical policy of preconceived exegesis: "seek and ye shall find." Both Blanshard and Edwards, unfortunately, apply it, methodically and with a vengeance.

For further discussion of SK as a predominantly *rational* thinker, see Paul L. Holmer, "Kierkegaard and Logic," *Kierkegaardiana* 2 (1957): 25-42.

possibility of a genuine and demonstrable form of faith, *as* faith, yet one just as interdenominational (nondenominational) as Edwards describes and countenances. In these cases, the sincerity and depth of character of the believer or aspirant are usually considered the sole standard of measurement (if that be the word) of religiosity; the content of beliefs is subordinate to testimony of the central role they play in organizing, unifying, and integrating the life-functions of the individual whose claims are under review or subject to litigation (e.g., in conscientious objector cases). As philosophical pragmatists in religion from William James to John Hick have contended, the crucial question is, do the beliefs "make a difference" in the life of the one they affect, and what *sort* of difference do they make, that is unique and could not for that person be duplicated or provided for by anything else? The major issue then is not *what* those beliefs are, but *how* they influence and guide the person maintaining them, in a distinctive way. These criteria are reasonable, intelligent, fair, and subject to little abuse, inasmuch as their verification takes place along many observable and reportable fronts (what SK would of course rule out as either impossible or untenable, in advance). They also allow learned justices to decide many a vexed question of personal fate with something approaching integrity, and with few loopholes for the escape of those who might either feign piousness, or be tempted to try.

Edwards's counter-example is therefore on reflection unimpeachable, even though it would, undoubtedly, fail to meet with SK's approval. There is no "outside" objective way for SK or a self-styled intellectual disciple to discriminate between religious man and infidel, between truth and falsity, between "edifying truth for you" and disedifying falsehood for me or for everyone. Such a means is necessary, if religion is responsibly to discharge its obligations to *itself*, let alone to man or society. The SK-ian stipulations concerning inwardness (*CUP* 232) resemble the Augustinian strictures on personal truth (*Confessions* 11. 3) in that they provide no method—rational or otherwise—for the resolution of disputes, some of which, as history shows, can escalate into wars and other destructive consequences. SK vehemently disapproves of crusading, that is, of attempting to impose religion on others, not only because that would violate the inwardness and "incognito" criterion that must be protected at all costs, but also because of its jejune presumptuousness over against other men (*CUP* 540). But, while SK's heart may be well-disposed, does he have an effective guard against religious excesses, all falsely committed "in the name of God"? I think not—although I wish this point had first occurred to Edwards, or Blanshard, instead of being left to me to disclose! SK reminds us that the man of true faith is not identifiable in public terms; he might just as well be a milkman or publican (*FT* 49), so undemonstrative is he. But is there not a difference between translucently noble religious personalities and unjustified, shallow, and insensitive bragging? Is it necessary to oppose the former in order unhesitatingly to condemn the latter? Are not *both* alike detectable to the trained (nondetached) observer, and also distinguishable from one another? Cannot the experienced (wise, humane) person detect a, or the, difference between genuine piety and compassion, and false or hypocritical coinage? Is this not a form of public knowledge, vouchsafed to everyone? I would judge so, at any rate.

Second, and far more damaging, if Christianity is not to be viewed historically, not as a series or collection of events, and if its relation to the individual believer is "decisively expressed" in ways that are inaccessible to public inspection and ratification, then how can Christianity (and it alone) be deemed *both* worthy of and capable of provoking the sentiment or feeling that is equated with or helps to define the requisite qualities for religiousness B? The claim that Christianity *ought* to inspire the individual who seeks to unify his experience *(CUP* 311, 365, 371) is normative, and indeed a proper part of celebration of the attainment in thought of an ideal of holiness; but the claim that it *does* so transform certain psyches is, again, irreducibly empirical, one that is open to confirmation (or disconfirmation) by some sort of observational means. Is Christianity then in its appearance and reappearance in the personal lives of various individuals, something that occurs utterly fortuitously? Or is there a true community of belief, with an identity founded, not on chance, but on a widely shared intuition, accompanied by concrete beliefs and practices? SK rejects the latter idea *(CUP* 49-50; *PF passim);* but how can unhistorical "inwardness" be called "Christian" each time (however seldom) that religiousness B takes hold of an individual, without raising a justifiable suspicion that this repeated human introjection of Christian principles is neither coincidental nor inexplicable, on the supposition of a cultural continuity of some kind, stretching across time? Denial strains against both plausibility and our precritical understanding that the *historical* event of the coming of the Messiah did *change* the world, regardless of whether one accepts the Messiah's status in the way that Christians do. It requires *no* "Leap of faith"[16] to recognize the real difference that

16. As Edwards very acutely maintains, worshipers of human deities (the State, or themselves, in the twin cases of political rulers and private narcissists), in short, idolators, would not be or constitute exemplifications of religiousness B to SK, because they ". . .are not in the truth even when their pitch of inwardness *(cf. CUP* 232) is 'infinite'. . .because the object of their infinite concern is not the infinite God but somebody finite and imperfect" *(KTC* 104). This enables SK in turn to *distinguish* between "genuine and aberrant inwardness," more or less successfully *(KTC* 104). For Edwards, this does *not* extend to believers in *other* religions (but what qualifies something as a religion?). I am inclined to agree, if only in hopes of lifting a more universal, less categorical lesson from SK than has hitherto been thought feasible.

This raises once more the hopelessly involved question (see esp. *CUP* 497-98) as to whether the somewhat faint criteria for religiousness B do include the existence

Christianity makes, or has made, in history; why, then, should a satisfactory account of faith disburden itself of something so useful, as well as so vital to its deepest aims? Why should the goals of faith be thought incompatible with a temporal analysis, when temporality is the half-concealed basis, as SK relentlessly insists, of human life?[17]

Unfortunately, Edwards never fastens on this problem. The cause of this is ignorance, ignorance of the master-disciple paradigm (itself a piece of Platonic and scriptural exegesis), which represents the movement toward faith in the *Fragments*. Responsible, too, is the blindness engendered by the one-sided approach toward religion that Edwards adopts. There are enough genuine inadequacies in SK's purported reconciliation of objective Christianity with subjective inwardness, although they are never ones simply

of God in some (nongross) external sense, or else whether (by some heaven-sent accident) the "Bish" intensity is instead prompted, and only prompted, by those sources which SK sets up as being ideal (and which *merge* inwardness with historical, community-of-believers-oriented Christianity, in another glorious incidence of happenstance). Edwards makes short work of this difficulty, yet he is not half wrong in concluding that ". . .a person [is] in the truth only if, in addition to feeling infinite concern, it is also the case that the object or objects appropriate to this infinite concern do in fact exist" (*KTC*, 105). Allowing for a liberal definition of "objects," which I am sure Edwards would permit, this makes much sense; Popkin takes a fundamentally similar line (in "Kierkegaard and Scepticism," repr. in Josiah Thompson, ed., *Kierkegaard: A Collection of Critical Essays*, pp. 371-72).

For a silly cheapening of the meaning of "leap of faith" (see also *KTC* 94 on this often overwrought point) to the level of a probabilistic calculation (*cf. CUP* 31, 485 and the *Fragments*), see Robert Paul Wolff, *The Poverty of Liberalism* (Boston: Beacon Press, 1968), p. 14n. Also see n15 here, above, on SK *vs.* Pascal.

17. The incompatibility suggested might be thought to stem from the antithesis between man's perishability and the "timelessness" of religious truths. But (a) SK derides the notion of timeless truth; (b) even a timeless truth could be apprehended by a time-bound creature, as examples drawn from mathematics unquestionably show. Besides, SK's objective is to show that there is no substitute for firsthand experience (*CUP* 147-63), to the point where secondhand information is considered unreliable, or no information at all. The trouble with this view is that even if true, the claims that derive from it (e.g., concerning religious faith) can never be *known* to be true, except in the (autobiographical) odyssey of personal discovery, which is of course disbarred from even attempting to communicate its experiences or insights. This seems a grave limitation, and unfair to the great literary traditions of mysticism, to cite just one possible counter-instance. (For critique of mysticism, see *E/O* 2: 250-53.)

to be ridiculed. The real, as opposed to phantom, problems of SK-ian scholarship include facing the prolixity and turgidity of the *Postscript* for what they are, yet continuing to emphasize the possibility of translation of their admittedly opaque messages into a clear, coherent, intelligible, and nonpartisan idiom. SK's "misguided epigoni" (a term employed by Mackey) have, as a rule, assumed that SK is best honored either by translating obscurities into the more obscure (instead of urging that they be given their "cash value," or its appropriate philosophical equivalent, in plain English—or plain Danish, as the case may be), or else by straitjacketing his insights into formal "existential" systems, which leaning SK expressly warned against and repudiated. Edwards is not guilty of either of these errors, but only, like Blanshard, of failing to abide by the scholarly norms, (i.e.), of not knowing the sources thoroughly, and of a certain irredeemable shallowness and insensitivity in interpretation, as well. Unfortunately, the latter qualities have become expected of Anglo-American philosophers, and neither Blanshard nor Edwards is disappointing in this respect.

VII: *Conclusion*

Kierkegaard had no doctrine; he ridiculed its appearance in Hegel *and* the hints of it that crop up in his own works. This does not entail, however, that his writings possessed no logic, no rationale, no structure, no *bona fide* purpose. What is valuable in SK does stand in need of supplementation; it is not in need of premature criticism, nor of reproach not founded on exquisite textual knowledgeability. The scholar's goal, under present circumstances, must be to dispel myth, and to reduce the quantity and pernicious effects of exaggeration and error, in reporting or commenting upon SK's views. SK is often hard to elucidate, and harder still to deal with in such manner as to lessen the extent of previously accumulated misunderstanding. But SK's writings will remain the repository for one of the most profoumd and moving of all accounts of the sufferings and struggle of the human soul, and, despite irregularities and unresolved difficulties that continue to plague the researcher attempting to clarify as well as justify the major theses of SK-ian thought, they shall always be intellectual milestones in their original and thoroughgoing effort to come to grips with the experiential tensions that constantly pull man between earth and eternity, between this life and the conjectural one to follow, between the roots and poles of finite and infinite, between himself and his ontological sources.

5

Who Is Nietzsche's Overman?

Introduction

Who was Friedrich Nietzsche? A German philosopher, born in 1844, the son of a Protestant minister, brilliant and introspective, but always frail and in poor health. Trained as a classical philologist, he made such a mark as a scholar specializing in the Homeric epics that in 1869 he was awarded his doctorate from Leipzig without benefit of examination and, on the strength of two published papers and the recommendation of one of his professors, became a full professor at Basel. He reisgned his university position ten years later, in 1879, owing to a combination of circumstances: dissatisfaction with academic life, personal distress, and recurrent bad health. Perhaps the formative event of these years was his service as a paramedical assistant at the front during the Franco-Prussian war (1870-71); he was wounded while attending to the sick, and in addition suffered what might be described as permanent emotional scars from witnessing the ravages of human conflict. Nietzsche soon entered into conflicts of his own; in 1872 he published his first book, *The Birth of Tragedy from the Spirit of Music*, and it was met with shafts of ridicule from the leading philologists of the day. They condemned it as impressionistic and unscholarly, but some forty years later it was universally hailed as the most insightful and profound study of the ancient Greeks that the nineteenth (or many a previous) century had produced. Nietzsche had no taste for such polemics, and as a result his literary output was quite slim during the time of his professional tenure. After he burst from the confines of his university position, free to wander to and from different European resorts, carefully nursing his physical constitution, he found the leisure and perhaps the mood conducive to writing; in the decade from 1879 to 1889, he turned out nearly all the works that have subsequently made him world famous: *Beyond Good and Evil, Genealogy of Morals, Thus Spake Zarathustra, Ecce Homo, The Anti-Christ*, just to name a few. This is not to say that Nietzsche was inert during the years spent at Basel; but his colleagues considered him an embarrassment and a failure, and while Nietzsche's mind was ever active, his publication was limited to such works as *Thoughts out of Season* (including the segment entitled "The Use and Abuse of History"), works that did not count as contributions to philology by any stretch of the imagination, and that, consequently, did nothing to hamper his already poor academic reputation in the university cloister. Freed from this choking atmosphere, Nietzsche was able to turn his interests in whatever direction he pleased, without having to worry about how his ideas would be received by the literary or scholarly establishment. In 1889, his activity was peremptorily interrupted by madness; he died eleven years later, at the turn of the century, in 1900, not knowing what audience or posthumously bestowed fame would await him; the victim of a tragic career, one filled with much suffering, both the intense personal suffering accompanying intellectual vision and observation of humanity, and the slights and mortifications brought home by those around him, who spread malicious rumors and unwarranted gossip concerning his allegedly irregular habits and standards of conduct.

Who is Friedrich Nietzsche? He is a philosopher who, though devoid of the elaborate machinery connoted by the term "system," grapples directly with all the problems most central to contemporary civilization: the advance of technology and its invasion of the human spirit; the contradiction between mass education and the democratic ideal, as by-products of the Enlightenment tradition, on one hand, and of cultural depression fused with petty, post-Metternichian tyranny, on the other; the hypocritical export of all of the worst features of European life, under the banner of "civilization," to countries rapidly being colonized and oppressed; and above all, the encroachment upon the individual by a thousand different yet related forces, all acting to suppress and dampen the expression of his true personality, the discovery of his own being—commerce, the newspaper, science, the idol of unlimited progress, money and material worship, mass taste, and institutionalized religion, to list only the most prominent.

For Nietzsche was first and foremost a master psychologist, although he is not recognized under that rubric in the modern world. His concern was always with isolating the belief-structures and animating principles governing the conduct of persons—not least the intellectuals and system-builders whose thought and influence pervaded Europe during the eighteenth and nineteenth centuries: Newton, Hume, Kant, Darwin, and so on. Nietzsche, like his great contemporary William James (with whom, so far as I know, he was unacquainted), mistrusted both reason and the claims of rationality. Like James again, he held that philosophers were inadvertent biographers of their own minds, and that every attempt to deal in a comprehensive fashion with the order and workings of a supposedly intelligible universe (or an objective moral realm for that matter) amounted to nothing but "a species of involuntary confession" on the part of its creator—a projection, to use the language made fashionable by Feuerbach's critique of Christianity, from the author's own mind to the world outside the framework of his own methods and ideas. It is virtually no exaggeration to maintain that in some sense, Nietzsche did not "believe in" objective truth, or rather that he tried to expose objective truth as a belief rather than as a putative reality—what he denigrated as a "mere philosopher's prejudice" in *Beyond Good and Evil*.

Throughout his life, Nietzsche was obsessed with the same set of problems; pick up any one of his works, open it almost at random, and the same issues, the same themes, the same treatment of the same dilemmas will be found. Nevertheless, not all of Nietzsche's ideas are equally controversial, or of equal importance. In this chapter, I have selected the concept of overmanhood *(der Uebermensch)* as my focus. I have done so for several reasons. First, I believe it is the most significant of all Nietzsche's contributions to philosophy; second, I consider it among the more accessible of his central categories; third, I think it has very much to say to us today. Before I can launch a full-scale discussion of the overman idea itself, I should like to make a few preliminary remarks on the besetting themes of Nietzsche's philosophy, things that may help to throw the issues of this chapter into sharper relief. In this manner, understanding of the purpose behind the introduction of the overman will be, I hope, advanced.

I mentioned that Nietzsche deals with all of the crucial problems of current life. Paramount among these issues is that of religion and, in particular, Christianity. "We Europeans" know, proclaims Nietzsche, that God is dead; that "nihilism stands at the door"; phrases to be explained a bit later on. But, while we know that Christianity has expired, Christianity and religion are not identical, or even coextensive; great civilizations have come and gone, so it stands to reason that while this one will perish, it will be replaced by something. But by what? We cannot say; the future is too difficult, too indeterminate to be predicted; yet, we cannot resist attempting to delineate its course, both because of intrinsic fascination and out of concern for the future of our own race—humankind, our descendants. What we can say is that replacing Christianity will not be easy. Christianity promised much (eternal salvation and happiness) and, like most promisers, redeemed little; consequently, civilization is in a state of emotional depression, caused by the discrepancy between promise and performance. The bottom has dropped out of society, or at any rate threatens to do so. Why is this? Because, according to Nietzsche, most people (the "herd") cannot live with the truth; they cannot accept it for what it is, and, if compelled to recognize it, it destroys their lives. For all his castigation of "the will to truth" as a "philosopher's prejudice," Nietzsche, perhaps inconsistently, staunchly maintains that "candor is the last virtue," the last virtue that "we Europeans," we who are intellectuals, that is, still hold. Candor—honesty—precludes us from attempting to uphold Genesis in the face of evolutionary theory, or Dante against Copernicus. Christianity is not merely false, it is obsolete, outmoded. But the whisper returns: what will replace it? And, if the majority are too weak to rely on their own intelligence, who will be strong enough to survive the decline of one value system before we witness the universal advent of another? It is at this juncture that the overman theory is pressed into service, coupled with the now-infamous distinction in "rank" (between nobility and herd) that Nietzsche posits to characterize, if not account for, differences in men, differences that will decide the fate, the survival, of the species.

And this brings us, quite logically, back to the dominant motif in Nietzsche's own thought structure: the elaboration of psychological or personality types, to be sure along lines favorable to the development of the conception that Nietzsche considers ideal. As early as the *Birth of Tragedy*, we see this notion in operation; for it is there that Nietzsche draws his celebrated distinction between the Apollonian (light, restrained, clear, balanced, rational, harmonious) and Dionysian (dark, brooding, violent, introspective, prone to excess, sexually aggressive) forces in the human soul, a distinction he as much elicits from as applies to Greek literature; suggesting further that the accomplishments of the Greek spirit were due to the maintenance of a very tenuous (and sometimes integrated) balance between the two antithetical elements rather than the (presumably artificial or, in Freudian terms, "neurotic") suppression or exclusion of one of them. In short, the achievements of the Greek (or any) spirit, both individual and collective, were not and could not be due to the waxing of one force at the expense of the other; both had to thrive, and indeed one stimulated or called forth its enemy or opponent as a necessary complement, so that the two might canalize the emotional and intellectual energies of the person (or community) they jointly constituted, only thereby lending themselves to productive works and outcomes. Fusion between the Apollonian and Dionysian factors is held to be impossible; but sterility or disintegration and collapse are the result of failure to bring the two into a cooperative, albeit unstable, relationship. Nietzsche began his career by insightfully analyzing the growth and decline of Greek tragedy in terms of this illuminating model; subsequently he learned to extend his results to more general spheres of interest, and to look at humanity and at civilization as a whole in these or similar terms.

It is arguable that Nietzsche's reading of history is simplistic, his concentration on certain features of Western history selective, arbitrary, and therefore distorted. It is certainly true that Nietzsche rarely if ever argues on behalf of any of his own views; whether they are defensible or not, *he* does not trouble to defend them. Nietzsche, like Heraclitus and like Bergson, but in different ways, does not argue; he merely asserts, categorically and with no tolerance for disagreement in outlook or perspective. The patient but critical reader must naturally extract whatever he can, and not dismiss the rest too hastily. This is most difficult to do in the case of Nietzsche's own value theory, insofar as he may be said to have one. Given Nietzsche's deprecation of the claims of rational ethical theory, it is not surprising that his own value scheme should be subjective, perhaps hopelessly so. But it is important to remember that Nietzsche's leading ideas, whatever they may be, ought not to be confused with the crude and simplified interpretations of them to which his writings are admittedly subject. For example, there is his notorious philosophy of "will to power": clearly, "power" functions in this context as self-mastery, very much akin to the Greek notion of *sophrosyne;* it is very far indeed from the picturesque but vicious exploitation of Nietzsche's views that the Nazis, not to mention Nietzsche's less inadvertent detractors, have performed. Power, like many a Nietzschean metaphor, is a pic-

turesque *ex*ternalization for a condition that is *in*ternal to
the individual soul. Unfortunately, not all of Nietzsche's ex-
positors have been gifted with sensitivity to Nietzsche's
semi-poetic idiom, and so his teachings have naturally become falsified.

I allude to this, not only in clarification of views I earlier
expressed on the range and scope of Nietzschean thought,
but also because it assists in explaining the contemporary
relevance of Nietzsche's ideas. Some of us may consider religion to be a "dead issue," or Nietzsche's dissection of the
remnants of Christianity a mere nineteenth-century trauma,
hence of historical interest only. Others may hold the problems engendered by man's search for objects of belief and
worship to be perennial, yet consider the phenomena too
vast, too forbidding in their complexity and, in the context
of contemporary secularism, perhaps even too remote to
admit of incisive latter-day treatment. I am not saying here
that Nietzsche's analyses still have much to offer us—that
would be correct but trite. I am saying that even if we ignore these dimensions of human experience entirely, at
least for provisional purposes of discussion, there is a welter
of instances that serve to confirm Nietzsche's prognosis of
the increased melancholy and unhappiness of present-day
life, quite apart from the effects brought on by the decline
(or the deflated pretensions) of the Christian world-view
and its intellectual-moral edifice. *Anomie*, "identity crises,"
the Bomb, experiments in drugs and in communal living;
the high divorce and suicide rates in Western countries;
these and many additional, overly familiar phenomena of
our time all testify to a deep and continuing malaise in
Western society. Nietzsche was not the only prophet of this
form of disease—Thoreau, Dickens, and Ruskin, and an
army of pre-Romantic thinkers, were at the vanguard of
makers of such predictions. But Nietzsche did specify a
cure (the overman, as a bridge between contemporary and

future or anticipated civilizations), albeit, as we shall see, one that he did not repose much faith in. Moreover, the remedy that Nietzsche offers looks remarkably like some antidotes currently favored by segments of Western youth. To suggest just one parallel, the recent upsurge of popular interest in the anthropological novels of Carlos Castañeda is a Nietzschean, if not a Nietzsche-inspired, occurrence. Castañeda's Yaqui Indian sorcerer, who exerts the fascination of many young people in Western countries today, is a man who is self-possessed (albeit with the help of hallucinogens and intoxicants of various sorts); he has seen through the hypocrisy of convention, and the errors of orthodoxy; he is his own pillar of emotional strength and support; even his perception of physical objects, hence of external reality, supplies a stark alternative to the stodgy and unimaginative ways of his innocent American interviewer and, later, initiate in sorcery. It would be going too far to champion the Yaqui as a man of temperance, but it is not hyperbole to opine that the aspirations of many of Castañeda's readers and would-be followers are oriented toward self-discovery and overcoming of the obstacles, barriers, and impediments that stand in the way of personal growth: the road to self-mastery, self-confidence, and self-expression. Now, Nietzsche's overman is a favored embodiment of all these traits, and a number of others besides; he is not a hero or a saint nor has he a need for heroes as a prop to bolster and motivate his own psyche. He is, in brief, the exemplification of a much-sought-after, precious, and little-attained affective commodity, in this or any era: maturity, above all, responsibility, both for and to himself. He is, in the argot of today, "together."

For this reason alone, Nietzsche's philosophy is worth an investigation. What makes his version of responsibility more complicated, hence more worthy of serious consideration, than many of its contemporary offshoots and popularizations (and I am not for a moment claiming that Castañeda writes with Nietzsche in mind, or with any knowledge of Nietzsche), is his coupling of overmanhood with allied notions such as "eternal recurrence" (perhaps the most foggy and, in the odious sense, metaphysical of all Nietzsche's categories) and "yea-saying." It would involve digression to take these notions up in detail; suffice it to say that for Nietzsche, as for Schopenhauer (1788-1860), whose philosophy exerted considerable influence on Nietzsche in his formative years, the choice we make—whether to survive or not—survive in the sense of ability to retain (and discover) our identity as persons, not survival in a crude physical or biological sense—is not a choice at all, but the surging and workings of a nonrational force (the "will"), one that is unobservable except in terms of its effects, and whose principal manifestations, apart from sexual drives, alike betray a struggle between what Nietzsche terms life-promoting and life-denying forces, respectively. This encounter is not simply a bout between optimism and pessimism, or between reason (the intellect) and will (the emotions); but it is at least that, and that is enough to enable us to comprehend Nietzsche even when (in spite of his "last virtue," candor, as exercised on the subject of history) he cannot bring himself negatively to conclude that the human race will not make it through its latest night of the spirit. For, in spite of the brittle, self-dissolving quality of the rational aspect of the human animal, forever building scientific and metaphysical castles in the air only to upset and destroy them, history does repeat itself—which means, ultimately, that the race continues, whether for better or worse (or neither). And this also means that in the end, the life-promoting forces prevail, whether they deserve to (and it is not a question of that) or not. Hence, while it may be futile to investigate whether there have been overmen in the past, there can be no doubt that there *will be* overmen in the future, nebulous though the future must seem from the ignorant vantage point of the present. There *will* be overmen, for there *must* be; but what—and who—will they be? What will they look like or resemble? This is the task of the next section to examine. I shall show, in what I hope will be considerable depth, what overmanhood is, who the chief candidates for the title or the role are, what further considerations about overmanhood intellectually animate Nietzsche, how they govern his formulations, and what credentials overmen must offer in fulfillment of their prospective candidacy.

The Overman

Let me first set forth criteria for overmanhood, prior to further discussion and examination. Nietzsche in effect specifies four criteria, four qualifications that amount to the necessary and sufficient conditions for possession of the overman state.[1] The four criteria may be labeled as follows:

1. Creativity in valuation
2. Pertinacity in belief and action
3. Kindness toward inferiors
4. Respect for equals

These four taken together define "overman" and indicate, indirectly, to what extent historical specimens do, or fail to, live up to some or all the criteria proffered.[2] (These criteria, which I propose to analyze in blocks of two apiece,

---

1. For discussion, see Martin Heidegger, "Wer ist Nietzsche's Zarathustra?" in *Vortraege und Aufsaetze* (Pfullingen: Neske Verlag, 1954); trans. Bernd Magnus in *Lectures and Addresses* (New York: Harper and Row, 1967), also in *Review of Metaphysics* 20 (1967): 411-31. Also see Heidegger's as yet untranslated study, *Nietzsche*, 2 vols. (Pfullingen: Neske Verlag, 1961).
2. For discussion, see esp. Walter Kaufmann, "Nietzsche's Admiration for Socrates," in his *Nietzsche: Philosopher, Psychologist, Antichrist*, 3rd ed. (New York: Random House, 1968), pp. 391-411.

are essential to overman status; but in addition, the overman should possess such personality traits as a sense of
humor,[3] and the ability to make friends; yet, while desider-
ates, these are not essential components of his make-up).

Qualifications (1) and (2) are not stated explicitly anywhere in Nietzsche's writings, not even in *Zarathustra*.[4]
They emerge, rather, from a consideration of what is implicit in all of Nietzsche's writings, but especially the fragments comprising *The Will to Power*, which I shall regard
as the central document for present purposes. The core of
Nietzsche's outlook is as follows:

Christianity, as stated before, is dying. It is dying because the belief-structure that it supports is toppling. The
belief-structure is crumbling, presumably, because of the
blows dealt it by the combined and ruthless forces of
rationalism: Hume and Kant; Darwin; the progress of natural science; the politics of "Enlightenment"; the seculariza-
tion of life, especially the more dominant urban life; and
other assignable causes, socioeconomic as well as intellectual, causes too numerous to mention.

What will replace Christianity? We cannot say, for we
cannot *see*. "Nihilism stands at the door,"[5] but nihilism is
only the last gasp of Christianity, its perverse but final outcome, the ultimate expression of Christianity's own internal, unsupported, and twisted logic.[6] It stands to reason
that there will be future civilizations, which will supersede

3. "Laughter, the golden (Olympian) vice;" *Beyond Good and Evil*, 294, trans.
M. Cowan (Chicago: Regnery, 1955), p. 232. Also see *The Will to Power*, §990, p.
517. (See full ref. below, in n4.)
4. Recall that "Zarathustra himself. . .is merely an old atheist. . . . Do not
misunderstand him;" *The Will to Power*, trans. Kaufman and R. J. Hollingdale
(New York: Random House, 1967), §1038, p. 535.
5. *The Will to Power*, 1, §1, p. 7.
6. *The Will to Power*, §5, p. 10, and §55, p. 35. Hence consciousness of
the internal contradictions lurking in Christianity renders it untenable, as expressed in the familiar (and overworked) theme: "God is dead." Belief is waning,
because it relies on a metaphysical and mythological structure whose inadequacies
the Enlightment has exposed.

our own, but their content is just a matter for speculation. We can imagine that the period between the decay of Christianity and the rise of its replacement, whatever that may turn out to be, will be long and painful. It is also likely to be an arid epoch, artistically and scientifically; for history allows us to examine several precedents (such as the era between paganism and Christianity, for instance) in confirmation of this pessimistic prediction.

Moreover, because of the peculiar nature and character of the Christian brand of belief and mythology, the decline of Christianity must pose a severe threat to the emotional health and well-being of mankind,[7] as much if not more so than was caused during the centuries of its unquestioned ascendancy. The question, then, is one of survival: *who* will survive the transition period between Christianity and that unknown, unnamed "X"? More significantly, *who* will provide the seeds for the planting of a new culture? *Who* will mold and transmit the undefiled and valuable elements from the old civilization, and how incorporate them within the as-yet indiscernible new one? Clearly, a new breed of individuals is required for this difficult and delicate task; a hardier race, emotionally and intellectually, than what the earth has spawned or witnessed thus far. For this reason, the idea of the overman is summoned forth by Nietzsche. Its introduction is explained by (1) Nietzsche's perception of the imminent dissolution of civilization as it is known, and (2) the desire to assure a future for mankind during the chaotic and troublesome period that will inevitably follow upon Christianity's inexorable demise.

Remarks. (a) Nietzsche exhibits a touching, if wholly gratuitous, concern for the welfare of future humanity. This belies those interpretations which seek to smear Nietzsche as the arch-defender and champion of personal (and politi-

---

7. Recall Nietzsche's imprecations about man as the "sick animal," and the accompanying biological metaphors, rampant throughout *The Genealogy of Morals.*

cal) cruelty, a theme that he usually discusses in connection with the Apollonian-Dionysian contrast.[8]

(b) In spite of his attacks on Darwin and Darwinism,[9] there can be no question that the notion of the overman is in some sense derivative from the more general evolutionary currents of thought that were prevalent during the second half of the nineteenth-century. Nietzsche is fond of saying that natural selection has gone in the diametrically opposite direction from that which would truly promote the maintenance of the species; that the weakest, not the strongest, are being bred, and that the human race is, consequently, bent on a headlong path toward its own destruction.[10] However, this is only to be rectified by a "transvaluation of all values," with Nietzsche's concomitant defamation (albeit, mixed with grudging admiration) of Jewish-Christian "slave morality."[11] It is clear to Nietzsche that, if humanity is to survive, it must go in the opposite direction from its predictably mediocre tendencies. In so doing, a new species, or "higher type," supposedly will evolve. Nietzsche does not deny, then, that there is an evolutionary process; he merely wants to harness it and to reverse what he takes to be its contemporary flow.

(c) The Nietzschean account is unavoidably impressionistic. Either you agree with Nietzsche's evaluations and predictions of the course of events, or you do not. It is fruitless to search for arguments in support of his main theses, and pointless to be dismayed at their absence. They stand (or fall) without benefit of scholarly apparatus or evidence to substantiate them.

8. The Will to Power, §801, p. 421.
9. See The Use and Abuse of History, trans. A. Collins, introd J. Kraft, 2d rev. ed. (Indianapolis, Ind.: Bobbs Merrill, 1957).
10. The Will to Power, §685, p. 364. Also see §921, p. 487.
11. The Will to Power, §172, pp. 103-4; "Christianity has grown out of psychological decay, could only take root in decayed soil," §438, p. 242 et passim. For some astute and appreciative observations, by way of contrast, see The Antichrist, §39. Kaufmann's comments on Nietzsche and (vs.) Darwin are valuable here; see his Nietzsche, p. 118.

From the foregoing we see the place of criteria (1) and (2), respectively. The overman must be capable of creating his own values, and of clinging to them ferociously and without vacillation. He must create his own world views, because the society around him is devoid of them, is morally and intellectually exhausted, indeed bankrupt; he must hold fast to them, ever aware that they are his values, his alone, and therefore subjective and arbitrary postulations. He must believe in them as firmly as though he were receiving the reinforcement of the world around him, which is (necessarily) lacking. He is isolated, on his own, all by himself. He must possess what Kierkegaard, in a fine phrase, calls "talent and authority":[12] Talent: the energy and ability to produce one's own rules of conduct, if rules there be; one's own minimal guide to life. Authority: the courage to maintain one's grip on the values one has set for oneself, in spite of universal opposition or lack of any encouragement. One must be creative, because the society no longer can provide useful or correct guidelines for the regulation of conduct; steadfastness, or faith in oneself, is requisite because one has no reliable external checks on the adequacy, or truth, of one's plan. When Zarathustra urges us to "break the old tablets"[13] he is not recommending vandalism, law-breaking, or even violence; he is pointing out that the old tablets have outlived their usefulness,[14] and that, in the interim between their destruction and the universal adoption of new proposals, the minds of individuals must support and sustain themselves, both in general and with regard to their specific courses of action.

12. Søren Kierkegaard, *Johannes Climacus: or, De Omnibus Dubitandum Est, and A Sermon*, trans. T. H. Croxall (Stanford, Calif.: Stanford University Press, 1958), pp. 134-36.
13. *Thus Spake Zarathustra*, trans. Kaufmann (New York: Random House, 1966), pp. 200, 205.
14. Much of Nietzsche's critique of Christianity is reminiscent of Feuerbach's strictures and indictments, a topic that would repay further exploration. For some concrete recommendations on how to go about the practice of overmanhood as a corrective to slave-morality, see *The Will to Power*, §462, p. 255, and also §909, p. 481.

Who, then, conceivably qualifies as fulfilling criteria (1) and (2)? Socrates, preeminently. Socrates created his own values—those of truth, unswerving intellectual rigor; and personal faith in his "divine sign" was part of his pertinacious opposition to the entire Athenian society, part too of his repeated attempts to elevate their standards to his level. Socrates needs no exterior props; his trust and confidence are well and exclusively placed in his own ability (professions of ignorance notwithstanding) to follow arguments wherever they may lead, to test and analyze them, to sift data, evaluate definitions and their consequences. The accusations that he corrupted the youth and did not believe in the gods of the *polis* are in a certain sense just, for he was a law unto himself, and obeyed external standards of propriety only incidentally. Even his decision to remain in jail and face death, as expressed in the *Crito*, is unconventional, for he does not regard death as the worst fate that can befall a man, and refuses to escape in the cowardly manner that was quite customary for certain victims of political persecution in his time. We must also remember that he virtually baited the jurors into the death-sentence at his trial.[15] His behavior in the face of calamity, his refusal to compromise with his own principles, to accept exile, or to run away from his (self-inflicted) legal punishment were all highly unnerving to the citizens around him, as the after-effects of his martyrdom showed; they are also perfectly consistent with the portrayal of Socratic asceticism offered us by Alkibiades in the *Symposium*. Add to this Socrates' characteristic passion for dispassionate argument, for example, in the *Phaedo*, where the subject is immortality, something that one hardly expects to see treated in an un-

15. The actual historical details are of course murky and hence controversial. The "Socratic problem" is not our concern; for Plato's *depiction* of Socrates is what matters to Nietzsche. See, e.g., "The Problem of Socrates," originally in *Twilight of the Idols* (*Werke*, ed. Karl Schlechta [Munich, 1955], 2:951-56).

prejudiced manner (for psychological reasons alone) during an inquiry conducted on the last day of a person's life,[16] and you acquire the consummate picture of the overman in the flesh, and in operation. It does not matter that the figure is a literary one; it serves just as well, for Nietzsche's purposes.

However, there are two further criteria, as I have already mentioned. Fortunately, Nietzsche is explicit about that. As he puts it, with his usual pungency,

> It would be completely unworthy of a more profound spirit to consider mediocrity as such an objection [to the appearance and flourishing of the overman]. In fact, it is the very *first* necessity if there are to be exceptions [overmen]: a high culture depends on it. When the exceptional human being treats the mediocre more tenderly than himself and his peers, this is not mere politeness of the heart—it is simply his *duty*.[17]

As Nietzsche equally warns against dire temptation elsewhere: do not spoil mediocrity for the mediocre.[18] Not if you cherish overmanhood, at any rate!

This raises the important question: who are the mediocre? The masses, the mob, those whom Nietzsche identifies deprecatingly as "the herd." What makes them mediocre? Is it the fact that they are not overmen? That would be a precise but unenlightening way to distinguish and identify them. Why are they not overmen? What pre-

16. Commentators like to point out that many of the demonstrations in the *Phaedo* are fallacious. But Socrates is very much aware of this, or else why his elaborate protest against the dangers of "misology" (89D)? *(Cf.* Kant, *Grundlegung zur Metaphysik der Sitten,* Prussian Academy ed., 4:395; *Groundwork of the Metaphysic of Morals,* trans. H. J. Paton, 3d ed. (New York: Harper & Row, 1964), p. 63.

17. *The Antichrist,* §57 (*The Portable Nietzsche,* trans. Kaufmann (New York: Random House, 1968), p. 647). Italics in text.

18. *The Will to Power,* esp. §§892-93, pp. 475-76. It is fair to retort that the overman depends on the good will and service of the community even if he refuses to recognize it—and them.

cludes this possibility? Only the fact that they are unable to handle (emotionally and intellectually) the devastation of their personal lives, as brought about (e.g.) by the decline of Christian civilization. They cannot live or get along without props, nor without the approval, the reinforcement of their peers. They are the *victims* of the insights bequeathed by the avant-garde, by the scientists and philosophers who have penetrated and exposed the "lie" of the web of belief comprising Christianity. Why victims? Why not celebrants? Because their life has been permanently disrupted, and they simply do not have the mental or emotional equipment at their disposal to repair it. Why victims? Why not co-discoverers? Because the knowledge has filtered down to them from on high, for example, from Hume's *Dialogues* and Kant's first *Critique*, indirectly, through the dissemination of knowledge to the public—a popularization that Nietzsche vehemently opposes, as he opposes all traces of "modernism" (equal rights, women's suffrage, newspapers, universal literacy) for hastening the demise of any society on which the Christian (or some other, equally serviceable) "lie" is founded. Moreover, the spread of information is itself a disservice to the public—it is an unkindness, as Nietzsche would say; and, borrowing the terminology of the ethico-religious tradition that he claims to have completely abandoned, Nietsche would add that it is the positive *duty* of the overman not to disturb the quietude of his "inferiors." This adds up to requirement (3). "For the mediocre, to be mediocre is their happiness."[19] Beware of troubling or upsetting it! Keep your 'wisdom' to yourself!

Nietzsche would, I take it, approve of the "quietism"

19. *The Antichrist*, §57 (*The Portable Nietzsche*, p. 647). Nietzsche places a premium on kindness to inferiors, hence on keeping the mediocre undisturbed, the ignorant uninformed. Not surprisingly, therefore, he characteristically lambastes Socrates for representing "a moment of the profoundest perversity" in the entire history of moral theory, seen from Nietzsche's standpoint. Nietzsche is most firmly a disbeliever in intellectuals engaging in "boat-rocking."

demanded, among other things, by Kant in "What is Enlightenment?" [1783]. It is *on* Nietzsche's plus-scale of values, and therefore must forthwith be part of the overman's stock-in-trade. Spinoza's action, too (if the story is not apocryphal), in telling a peasant woman who had inquired into the possibility of salvation in her religion that she could be saved in any religion, provided she be pious and go about her business unruffledly, would win Nietzsche's applause—as would Spinoza's saving his "atheism" for his books, leaving them to be published after his death, and to be distributed and discussed only among the learned. (The persistent legend of secret, oral teachings in Plato's Academy might hold a similar charm and—with respect to Socrates—a very special appeal).

But what about Socrates? Socrates does not pass the test at this point, although his context is pagan rather than Christian. In dialogue after dialogue, Socrates is notorious for spoiling mediocrity for the mediocre. It is small wonder that Callicles fumes at him, that Anytus warns him, that Meno reproaches Socrates for being a "sting-ray," reminding him that he would be denounced as a wizard and condemned to die, in the town where Meno hails from. (And, as it happens, this comes about anyway, even in Athens). Disturbingly, too, the essentially aporetic quality of the early Socratic discourses stands as another permanent violation of an overman canon. Moreover, there is not to be overlooked criterion (4): the recognition of other overmen as being overmen, and consequently as deserving of deferential treatment. This reveals Nietzsche's preoccupation with equality: not general human equality, which Nietzsche unhesitatingly castigates as "the greatest of all lies,"[20] but the equality "in rank"[21] of the superior minds and spirits.

20. *The Will to Power*, §464, p. 256.
21. *The Will to Power*, §875, p. 468; §881, p. 470; §882, p. 471; §935, p. 493; §961, p. 504; §999, p. 519.

For, as Nietzsche stresses, nobility demands "the conviction that one has duties only to one's equals, toward the others one acts as one thinks best: that justice can be hoped for (unfortunately not counted on) only *inter pares*,"[22] or from fellow overmen, one's colleagues, as it were.

Does Socrates recognize his peers as peers? Who are his peers? The Sophists, no doubt. They, too, are rugged individualists of a sort; they postulate their own values, and maintain them in the face of objections and political difficulty. We recall that Protagoras dared to visit Athens in spite of his bad reputation and the personal jeopardy in which he was placed, that Gorgias, to rebut criticism, protested to Socrates his own innocence as a mere rhetorician, one not to be held responsible for the mindless abuses of any evil-intentioned but ever-crafty students. Never mind that the Sophists preach success rather than goodness, and take a fee for their services. They are the first real teachers in Greece, not counting Homer; they establish a precedent for Socrates' own concern with ethical topics, with personal (and civic) excellence; they are acutely conscious of the decline of Periclean democracy, and of its effects on neighboring city-states, and are able to manage their own affairs in spite of the precipitous decline in public morality (indeed, are able to turn it to their own advantage); they seemingly thrive in the face of opposition from large and influential segments of the public; and, above all, they make a generous contribution to the intellectual climate of the times,[23] one that provides the milieu for Socrates' own undertakings.

It is of course arguable whether Socrates did or did not treat them (1) respectfully and (2) as they deserved! Point

22. *The Will to Power*, §943, pp. 496-97. Italics original. Observe too that "Not 'mankind' but *overman* is the goal" *(The Will to Power*, §1001, p. 519).
23. For full study, see W. K. C. Guthrie, *A History of Greek Philosophy*, vol. 3 (Cambridge: Cambridge University Press, 1969).

(1) depends on one's interpretation of the appropriate dialogues; point (2), on how closely one allies Socrates to the Sophists, after first allowing for Plato's numerous literary attempts to dissociate Socrates from them, both in the *Apology* and elsewhere. However, it is noteworthy that in at least one dialogue *not* about a Sophist, Plato's chief protagonist encounters more than his match: I am referring to the *Parmenides*, where Socrates is improbably represented (a) as being a philosopher, yet only 20 years of age, and (b) as affirming a version of the Theory of Forms. Nevertheless, it is interesting to observe that Parmenides, while demolishing the Theory of Ideas throughout the dialogue and making Young Socrates appear thoroughly amateurish and clumsy in his defense and articulation thereof, treats his interlocutor with utmost courtesy, a courtesy that is neither feigned nor perfunctory, and that bespeaks a deep awareness on Parmenides' part (in contrast to his shallow, eristically oriented lieutenant, Zeno) of the "talent and authority" lurking inside his dialectical adversary. (The credit for the dramatic presentation of the events must of course go to Plato, the more so as the rencontre itself did not, in all likelihood, ever take place).

In any case, even if Socrates stands up to requirement (4), the Socratic conversations make failure to live up to Nietzsche's criterion (3) all too abundantly evident. So Socrates comes close, but is not an overman, for he imposes on his inferiors in a way that Nietzsche is compelled to find distasteful and repugnant—not to mention, boat-rocking. (See n19, above).

Jesus Christ, another overman candidate, fails for similar reasons, although there is fertile ground for textual controversy on some points.[24] He may indeed be pertinacious, but it is doubtful whether, in Nietzsche's eyes, he qualifies

---

24. Kaufmann devotes a chapter of his fine book to this problem, so I shall not dwell on it at length here. See his *Nietzsche*, pp. 337-90.

as original, inasmuch as his moral teachings allegedly embody the psychological culmination of the "Jewish ethic." Moreover, he has no peers—could the Son of God admit of equals?—and this disqualifies him automatically, since Nietzsche's overman is certainly not "superman," at least not in the sense of being supernatural in origin or powers. And it is not at all clear that Jesus treats his inferiors— which means everybody else—with kindness. His kindnesses are numerous, but his malicious glee at the prospect of his enemies getting their just desserts is chilling, and his one-upmanship with Peter as well as Pilate is both consistent and consistently appalling. One would be remiss not to add that Nietzsche repudiates Christ's reliance on human weakness and frailty ("the last shall be first"), as opposed to building on the strength and internal conviction that radiate from the mind and soul of a Socrates. Socrates comes closer to fulfilling the Nietzschean ideal, although in the end he, too, fails. Who is Nietzsche's overman? No one.[25]

Conclusion

It is time now to step back and examine the cumulative outline of the overman as just presented. On final evaluation, first it appears as a disguised model of human excellence. "The will to power" is just another way of designating the ancient *arete*, or better still, *arete* coupled with one of its principal components, *sophrosyne*, as commendable paradigms for human conduct. Nietzsche's overman conception takes its place alongside Aristotle's *phronimos* or *spoudaios*, Butler's cool man, Smith's ideal observer, and the like; the differences between the specific conceptions of moral excellence may be vast, but the overall heading

25. "Never yet has there been an overman." *Thus Spake Zarathustra*, trans. W. Kaufmann (New York: Viking, 1966), p. 93. Presumably this is a self-inclusive statement, both contextually *and* autobiographically.

amounts to the same. It is this that qualifies Nietzsche as an ethicist, and not as a mere "astute social critic"; he *is* a profound observer of human nature, but also much more than that, despite the deliberate absence of "system" or ratiocinative structure from his compositions.

Second, from our vantage point it is now possible fully to appreciate the force of Nietzschean pessimism as well as of Nietzschean optimism.[26] The pessimism stems from the failure even of potential overmen to fulfill all of the Nietzschean demands. This is one major reason why Nietzsche's work is abortive, why his philosophy remains "incomplete," quite apart from the tragic interruption of his early madness. There is no point in detailing the vision of the future if that future is itself in doubt. (This may also explain why Nietzsche's obscure doctrine of "eternal recurrence" was never elaborated.) On the other hand, if the human race is to last (emotionally and mentally, not just physically) the mysterious and perilous transition, it *must* develop, to show the overman traits just sketched. Hope is therefore the only rational attitude possible, for without it, all is lost, and replaced by a mixture of fear, despair, defeat, and resignation. This is why, though Nietzsche's mature, evolutionary yet cyclical philosophy of history is "unfinished," there remains something to do, some refinement for the reader to glean from the ongoing labor of interpretation. Therefore, as scholars approach the ever-renewed task of clarification and the activity of engaging in fresh exegesis, our own project should always be borne in mind, as a contribution to

26. See esp. *The Will to Power*, §463, p. 255. Note that Nietzsche is only too well aware that he himself does not possess the transcending attributes of the overman; he is rather like Faust, frustrated and unhappy but held in chains by candor, by "the last virtue"; by *truth*, the dogma and prejudice that "we Europeans" subscribe to uniformly, as *Beyond Good and Evil*, §1-2, §43-44, trans. M. Cowan (Chicago: Regnery, 1955), pp. 1-3, 48-51. asserts. I would therefore insist that in the end, Nietzsche, scholar that he is, is no better (or better situated, pathologically speaking) than the herd whom he despises and is openly contemptuous of. And I think he knows and accepts this.

the cumulative progression of insights on the topics of central concern befalling every philosopher of the human condition.[27]

27. I am indebted to D. Temple for stimulating and valuable discussions that prompted my initial research on this chapter.

6
Against the Logicians:
Some Informed Polemics

K*ant* remarked[1] that logic had not made a single advance since the time of Aristotle. Indeed it had not, although in the nineteenth and twentieth centuries it did make enormous strides. But progress is sometimes confusing, and, in the case of logic, progress has been made in spite, not because of such confusion. We have witnessed on the one hand the growth of mathematical logic (sometimes called "formal" or "symbolic" logic), growth that even in scientific annals is virtually unparalleled, while on the other

1. *Critique of Pure Reason*, Bviii.

hand, the last two centuries have seen successive attempts at grand-scale, metaphysically oriented revision. Dating from Hegel, and continuing through Lotze, Bradley, McTaggart, and the remaining members of the British Idealist school, the history of recent philosophy has been punctuated by the appearance of gigantic tomes, each of which promises, first, to change our thinking about logic, and second, to install this newly altered conception of logic as the pivot for a brand-new mode of philosophizing. Invariably, such revision of the notion of logic (and, consequently, of the very use to which the term "logic" is put) winds up trailing large clouds of vaporous metaphysics behind itself. What happens subsequently involves a rapid exchange of fire between the mathematical logicians and the metaphysicians, which is then followed by prolonged bouts of silence on each side.

This describes the case even today. We have on one side the experts at symbol-manipulation, the masters of technique; and on the other, those old "muddle-headed" nontechnical philosophers (e.g. Ryle, Toulmin) who still dare to raise their voices in criticism, who practice "informal" as opposed to symbolic logic. One hears oneself adding in a whisper, "and never the twain shall meet." This is a sad situation for all concerned. Can anything be done to alleviate it? Or are we destined to remain divided between the respective practitioners of mathematical and "philosophical" logic, the latter often uninformed by, and uninterested in, the developments occurring in and transforming the former?

I think that it is not necessary for events to continue as they have been up to now, and I likewise believe that it is possible for a fruitful interchange of ideas to take place. Toward that end, the present essay is devoted. I shall examine a few selected issues that I consider to possess exploratory possibilities that hitherto have remained undeveloped.[2] These are issues that emerge simply from an examination of aspects of mathematical logic itself: the way in which it is presented as a discipline, as well as the manner in which the subject is as a rule taught. I shall offer criticism and "pragmatic" commentary thereon, but shall be guided throughout by the provisional conviction that what is under discussion is valuable philosophically, apart from its extra-philosophical initial merits as an examination of mathematical logic.[3]

Let us begin by looking at an obscure yet typical example of a modern, analytically-oriented critique of an alternative or traditional mode of philosophizing: one that accused John Dewey, the classical pragmatist, of neglecting such topics as the semantic definition of the horseshoe, the proper and improper construals of "entailment," and so on, all of which are standard fare in mathematical logic. The author of this attack, Marcus Singer, concludes that Dewey's use of the term "logic" is hopelessly idiosyncratic, that Dewey's major book on the subject is sloppily constructed, inadequate, and incomplete with respect to what Singer deems logically important.[4]

How does one reply to such charges? It is true that Dewey's conception of logic is, by present standards, highly bizarre, for Dewey's work stems from just that revisionist metaphysical tradition whose intellectual roots are in Hegel, whose several prominent representatives have differed among themselves as to how to define "logic" and, more significantly, as to what philosophical capital to derive from

2. Precisely for this reason I shall largely ignore both modal and combinatory logics, since their philosophical potential has already been widely recognized and since they have already undergone considerable scrutiny.

3. This conviction is forcibly argued against by Henry B. Veatch, in his *Two Logics* (Evanston, Ill.: Northwestern University Press, 1969).

4. M. G. Singer, "Formal Logic and Dewey's Logic," *Philosophical Review* 60 (1951): 375-85.

their activity. The unsettled nature of philosophic controversy in general is such that it permits Singer to poke
fun at Dewey, and to exploit to the fullest Dewey's personal handicaps, notably his twisted syntax, numerous ob-
fuscations, and characteristic ambiguity and imprecision.
Dewey tries to defend himself from such attacks in advance
by observing that

> in the present state of logic, the absence of any attempt
> at symbolic formulation will doubtless cause serious ob-
> jection. . .this absence is not due to any aversion to such
> formulation.[5]

But, Dewey continues, without being grounded in a comprehensive theory of language and of experience,

> formal symbolization will. . .merely perpetuate existing
> mistakes while strengthening them by seeming to give
> them scientific standing.

In short, Dewey here pleads for philosophy as a prerequis-
ite for doing symbolic logic properly. This only compounds
the problem, however, in the eyes of Singer and many
other logicians. Philosophy in their view is "on trial" for its
previous failures,[6] and can no longer proceed unless it is
formulated clearly and precisely—which means, unless
philosophic discourse is carried on only under the control-
led conditions of an artificially constructed language, as
Tarski, Carnap, Bar-Hillel, and others envision it.
Moreover, philosophy, if it is to be done at all, is to be
done *after* and not before the erection of such a language;
criticism is devoid of meaning unless it takes place within a
linguistic framework (this is part of what Quine has in mind

5. J. Dewey, *Logic: The Theory of Inquiry* (New York: Holt, 1938), p. iv. The
succeeding quotation is from the same page.
6. This of course is a markedly unfair *tu quoque;* Dewey himself brings it up
elsewhere, in *Experience and Nature*, 2d ed. (Chicago: Open Court, 1929), pp.
410ff, as a weapon of social critique and indictment.

in speaking of "ontological relativity," which means, relativity with respect to a chosen morphology or a logical vocabulary).

It is easy to see why relations between logicians and philosophers are more than a bit strained after a series of such encounters. It is also easy to perceive the malicious glee on the part of logicians, who enjoy twitting philosophers such as Dewey for their sheer *inability* to carry on their investigations under the terms laid down for them by the logicians. To prevent a complete breakdown in communication, the only thing that can be done is to try to meet the logicians on their own terms, but without succumbing. As Whitehead pointed out in his lecture on "Mathematics and the Good," exactness is a fake. Aware of this stricture, let us nonetheless obey the conditions proposed by many logicians, as a temporary expedient or conversational ice-breaker, and see what develops.

1. *Use and Mention.* Mates correctly observes that "the use-mention distinction is absolutely essential for understanding modern treatments of logic."[7] However, many logicians approach it as if grasping (and consistently employing) it were of paramount importance in the actual pursuit of knowledge. This is quickly given the lie by the fact that even so original a piece of research as the recent landmark study by P. J. Cohen contains frequent violations of the use-mention dichotomy in the area of domains. So far as we know, no earth-shaking logical paradoxes have materialized from Cohen's failure (typical of mathematicians) to observe throughout such theoretical niceties, nor is his book's mathematical worth in any way diminished by such minor sloppiness.[8] This means that, like it or not, use *vs.* mention belongs, not to mathematics but to philosophy, and is a re-

7. B. Mates, *Elementary Logic* (New York: Oxford University Press, 1965), p. 19.

8. P. J. Cohen, *Set Theory and the Continuum Hypothesis* (New York: Benjamin, 1966).

flection on outcomes rather than a necessary tool for doing competent work.

What *is* the use-mention distinction? The terminology itself comes from Quine, who credits its explicit introduction to Frege and then, later on, Carnap.[9] The distinction enables us to differentiate between two kinds of functions that an expression may have: to name an object, or to refer to itself. To attempt glibly to define the distinction is not easy; to show the apparent need for some such device is much simpler. Let us take a concrete example:

Fordham is 130 years old   (S)
Fordham is a 7-letter word   (T)

Clearly, there is a difference in the way in which the term *Fordham* is handled in sentences (S) and (T), respectively. In (S) it refers to a university, or to an organization or corporate body possessing certain characteristics, such as having been founded on a certain date or existing at a certain location. In (T) we are not talking about any of this, but about the linguistic entity "Fordham." Hence it is necessary for (T) to be rewritten as

"Fordham" is a 7-letter word,   (T')

lest (T) be called, in logician's terminology, not-well-formed. Note that (S) and (T) possess the same truth-value (i.e., both sentences are true), but for entirely different reasons, reasons not explained merely by the presence of the same token, namely *Fordham*, in each of them.

Now, in cases of ordinary usage, the use-mention distinction is usually not called for, inasmuch as one is rarely trip-

9. W. V. O. Quine, *Mathematical Logic*, rev. ed. (Cambridge, Mass.: Harvard University Press, 1951), p. 26.

ped up as a result of failing to heed it.[10] In symbolic logic, the situation is different, and so it becomes imperative to handle cases in which inability to distinguish use from mention with the naked eye, so to speak, must be prevented, and on a uniform basis, or else certain contradictions and paradoxes may arise. Even if this were no real danger, the use-mention dichotomy would still deserve its place. In an expression such as

$$p \supset q \qquad\qquad\qquad (X)$$

the three symbols employed are all drawn from what is known as the "object-language," that is, the (formalized) language that is under investigation or that is being manipulated or learned. However, in order to state general theorems concerning this object-language, it is necessary to resort to a "meta-language" (this terminology is originally Carnapian), which is constructed for the express purpose of formulating proofs concerning certain formal properties of the object-language, that is, in order to establish that the object-language must (or cannot) have these (dis)provable properties, which, typically, include soundness, consistency, completeness, and compactness. It may (and does) happen that in this meta-language one wishes to state, corresponding to (X) above, something much more general, namely

$$A \supset B \qquad\qquad\qquad (Y)$$

Unfortunately, while "A" and "B" are drawn from the meta-language, the horseshoe is not. Expression (Y) is thus a strange kind of hybrid, having (for the moment) no logical status of any kind, being neither sanctioned nor censured.

10. Except in some (humorous?) instances, as illustrated by the following common repartee:

> Wife: Say you love me, dear.
>
> Husband: You love me, dear.

On this occasion, the spouse's failure to study logic could prove to be a marital undoing! (For a further illustration of use-mention in action, see Appendix to chap. 6.)

Clearly, what is needed is a *rule* that will permit the entry of expressions such as (Y), or else some amendment of the formulae themselves that will enable them to be counted as well formed.

Historically, the responses to this problem have come in three versions. Quine introduced *quasi-quotation* (also known as "corners") to serve as a kind of signal that the formula in question combines symbols from two different morphologies.[11] Thus he would have us make a slight change in (Y), to read it as

$$[A \supset B] \qquad\qquad\qquad (Y')$$

before countenancing or including it (formulae such as (X) would remain untouched by such procedure).

A simpler proposal came from Church, who unsurprisingly credited its original introduction to Carnap.[12] This involves setting up a correspondence between symbols that are drawn from object- and meta-language, respectively, such that connectives (including the horseshoe, of course) could be used freely in both places; more particularly, the horseshoe as occurring in (Y') above could be said to denominate the horseshoe in (X), just as A and B themselves range over (and hence stand for) p and q, respectively. This would do away with the need for quasi-quotation, enabling us to go back to (Y) and so dispense with a cumbersome piece of extra notation.

Curry took the additional step of bringing connectives such as the horseshoe directly into the meta-language, thus doing away with the need even to consider the problem as posed.[13] This method of resolution is known as "radical usage," since the horseshoe symbol in the meta-language does *not* have to correspond to its identical configuration in the object-language, nor to any other item therein, for that

11. Quine, *Mathematical Logic*, pp. 33ff.

12. A. Church, *Introduction to Mathematical Logic* (Princeton, N.J.: Princeton University Press, 1956), 1:61, 63.

13. H. B. Curry, *Foundations of Mathematical Logic* (New York: Van Nostrand, 1963).

matter. So Curry, like Church, would say that (Y) is well formed as it stands, although each author makes separate provisions for surmounting the obstacle encountered.

What, it may well be asked, is the philosophical significance of all this?

The answer lies in the "commitment" that use *vs.* mention asks us to make. Logicians sometimes try to pretend that such commitments, if any, pertain only to the particular way in which a given dilemma is resolved. Thus, it is clear that Quine's method has no implications whatsoever, since it merely demands that we flag down or mark hybrid occurrences where and whenever we find them, while Curry's avoids commitment through an even simpler expedient. Meanwhile, Church's method, while preferable to Quine's in terms of ease of manipulation (but not to Curry's, whose outcome is the same in practice), does indeed "commit" us to a very austere brand of Platonism (so-called) in which abstract entities (in this case, logical connectives) on one level are held to reflect, in a one-to-one correspondence, the presence of such entities on another, controlling level. In short, there is a "form" of horseshoe; and, lo and behold, this form turns out to be a horseshoe itself—or perhaps it would be better to say, a horseshoe of horseshoes, or simply a capital-H Horseshoe. Both Curry and Church manage to evade committing themselves to the existence of an "idea" of horseshoe, each in their separate ways.[14]

But the real commitment lies elsewhere. For one thing, the whole concept of use and mention creates the impression of a hierarchy. This impression is confirmed, if indeed the whole question is not begged in advance, by the creation of meta- and object-languages, respectively, which creep onto the scene suddenly and quite unannounced. The

14. At this point, the unspoken implication is that it is "bad" to be committed at all, or, as Casimir Lewy reportedly once put it, that "no one wants to be a Platonist." This remark is very telling about the present-day philosophical atmosphere both in the United States and Britain.

complex of rules and overarching language structures does not end there, but proceeds upward indefinitely, as Carnap's experience can eloquently testify.[15] The English language is in most cases the "metametalanguage" in which instruction in formal logic is carried out. So it is hardly astonishing that we should be faced with the roles that a word such as *Fordham* can play, and be required, within an already elaborate framework, to make a clean breast between its "use" (as in [S]) and its "mention" (as in [T]). Platonism certainly is as rife here as anywhere else, both in the orderly layering of language upon language in a never-ending series (which begs for an arbitrary terminus, a language of languages, namely, Carnap's L, one to coordinate and superintend all the rest; something to function as surrogate for the Good, no doubt), and in the rigid delineation of the possible functions that can be played by given expressions.[16]

Moreover, modern logicians act as though they were the first to discover that a need for a device like use and mention existed. The medievals knew this; they preferred to distinguish between *suppositio formalis* and *suppositio materialis* instead (this is recognized by Church,[17] who nonetheless considers the distinction inadequate for the purposes at hand). The most fully developed and worked-out Scholastic theory is found in the until very recently neglected writings of William of Sherwood.[18]

---

15. See R. Carnap, *Der logische Aufbau der Welt* (1928), trans. R. A. George as *The Logical Structure of the World and Pseudoproblems in Philosophy* (Berkeley and Los Angeles: University of California Press, 1967).

16. It is of course quite easy to multiply the layers of use and mention, respectively, to an indefinite extent. Example: *Fordham* denotes "Fordham" (and so on, without any end).

17. Church, *Introduction to Mathematical Logic*, 1:61n.

18. William of Sherwood, *William of Sherwood's Introduction to Logic*, ed. N. Kretzmann (Minneapolis: University of Minnesota Press, 1966), and *William of Sherwood's Treatise on Syncategorematic Words*, ed. N. Kretzmann (Minneapolis: University of Minnesota Press, 1968). For discussion, see W. Kneale and M. Kneale, *The Development of Logic* (Oxford: Clarendon Press, 1962), pp. 231-34, 246ff.

I hold no brief for the Schoolmen; the point has rather to do with how, for philosophical if not for logical purposes, one may construe the relevant differences. As Dewey remarks in the earlier citation, what we really want is nothing less than a general theory of language. If we cannot ever have it free from the prejudices of rival philosophic camps (one has only to think of the recent efforts expended by J. L. Austin and R. M. Hare), at least let it not be prematurely swayed or affected by the methods employed by mathematical logicians. Dewey, for example, would, if he had only taken an interest in the matter, certainly have sided (for once!) with the medieval outlook, since it is so much closer to his own. For, William of Sherwood's claim is that when we say

Man is a rational animal   (Z)

or

Man is monosyllabic,   (ZZ)

what is manifested in each case is just a different *use* of the term "man," which is exemplary of nothing other than the "varieties of linguistic experience," to paraphrase James. The use-mention theorist, however, would compel us to accept a doctrine of radical differences in kind, so much so that when we mention the term "man" instead of using it, we are in effect using a term altogether unlike the word "man," all similarity of appearance between the two tokens notwithstanding.[19] The presence of single-quote marks (or in Quine's case, of quasi-quotes) magically converts any given word into a wholly novel term. Unrestricted application of such a principle quickly leads to one overwhelming difficulty, whose dimensions were fully faced by Kant in the

19. Thus William's contention, that ultimately it is a difference in terms of *usage* that is at stake, can still be maintained.

"schematism": namely, just how do abstract categories relate to their sensuous content; and this is in turn but one (very elegant) way of bringing up the classic Parmenidean one-many issue all over again.[20] Logicians, beware of metaphysics!

As soon as it has been recognized that the standard response of logicians to the contrast exemplified above in (Z) and (ZZ) is just *one stipulation* among many possible (and viable) means of accounting for and disposing of the perceived disparities, the ubiquitousness of use-mention, and the overwhelming rigidity of all modern approaches that we encounter there shall have been successfully challenged. This does not mean that the medieval approach is trouble free: for, what are we to make of the fact that, while (Z) is true by dint of a property shared by human beings as human, (ZZ) is true in virtue of a linguistic accident—to be sure, an attribute belonging to the word for man, but having nothing to do with humans themselves? But if this is a grave problem, it is certainly no *more* of one than those engendered by more currently desired methods of resolving it.

I shall next examine the contrasts between this new-found tolerance for a "loose" manner of resolution, and inflexible logical styles, as they again display themselves in treatments of the controversial philosophical problem of relations.

2. *Relations.* Are relations "real"? Leibnitz thought not; he attempted to reduce them to complex properties, but without success. By a relation, I simply mean a two-termed predicate, such as "north of," or "cousin to," or "partner of," or "adviser to," and so forth. To symbolize relations I shall employ variables plus a general function; thus, $\emptyset xy$ will here stand for any two-termed predicate whatsoever.

---

20. Whereas William's anticipation of instrumentalism altogether does away with such "untenable dualisms" (to use the damning phrase that first Dewey and then Morton White coined.)

Can relations be reduced to properties? Had Leibnitz lived in the twentieth century, he would have been overjoyed, for the answer is Yes, at least insofar as logic is concerned. By treating relations as the union of ordered pairs of unit classes, N. Wiener in 1914 established a method whereby relations can be systematically eliminated from the primitive syntax of logical systems.[21]

Does this mean that relations do not "exist," or that they are "unreal" in some sense, figments of our imagination, illusory or delusory? Of course not. To say that Jack and Jill are married is not to say anything that can be stated without having to refer to both parties; similarly, to scrutinize a ternary relation, that St. Louis is between Milwaukee and Little Rock, is not something that can be affirmed without involving all three cities in the declaration. '$\emptyset abc$' cannot be rendered equivalent to '$\emptyset ab$' or to '$\emptyset bc$' alone, not to mention reduction to some complex property Pb. Yet in pure logic, this can be done, and *is*, as a matter of routine.

Presumably, the philosophic motivation behind any attempted reduction stems from a deep-seated desire to behold the world monistically; in Sir Isaiah Berlin's classification, Leibnitz would fit admirably as one of the "hedgehogs."[22] There is also a more modest but powerful gain to be made: if "betweenness" can somehow be dissolved into a two-termed relation and thence into a property, it makes the actual task of verifying statements much easier. To mention one subject where such hopes are being entertained, consider biology; through advances in genetic coding it may well become possible to determine paternity of children born out of wedlock without any specific informa-

21. See N. Wiener, "A Simplification of the Logic of Relations," reprinted in J. van Heijenoort, ed., *From Frege to Goedel: A Source Book in Mathematical Logic, 1879-1931* (Cambridge, Mass.: Harvard University Press, 1967), pp. 224-27. For discussion, see C. I. Lewis, *A Survey of Symbolic Logic* (Berkeley and Los Angeles: University of California Press, 1918), pp. 269ff.

22. I. Berlin, *The Hedgehog and the Fox* (New York: Simon & Schuster, 1953), pp. 1-2.

tion in hand concerning the father's identity. A universal method for settling disputes reliably was what Leibnitz had in view, while lost in research over his projected *calculus ratiocinator*. Biology might make it come true, eventually!

However, there are times when a more directly metaphysical form of wish-fulfillment can also intrude. Suppose we look at the case of C. S. Peirce, who, while he anticipated so many of the later developments in formal logic, also came to the rescue of relations, fighting on behalf of their indispensability and irreducibility on philosophical grounds, while predicting their demise and replacement through results of his own mathematical research.[23] But, while Peirce argued that dyads and triads cannot be logically dissolved, he also held that all higher (that is, quaternary and above) relations can be made over into combinations of less complicated elements. (Structurally, this is slightly reminiscent of the psychological atomism of Russell, and before him that of Locke and Hume.) But why is the reductive urge so strong in a pragmatist such as Peirce, and why does this concern yet end in conflict with his equally fierce defense of the reality of relations (2- and 3-termed types only)?[24]

I believe that making the correct reply to all this depends on courageously making a counterintuitive separation of my own, (to my knowledge) unassayed before by anyone: namely, that between symbolic logic and philosophy there is no common ground. This procedure is shocking, yes, but also more defensible than to attempt either to extend the findings of logic itself to regions where they become patent absurdities, or else to controvert those accomplishments, which *are* valid on their own ground, by giving out discursively philosophical arguments, which, as seen before, are frequently very shaky, hence legitimately criticized for

23. For full study, see M. Murphey, *The Development of Peirce's Philosophy* (Cambridge, Mass.: Harvard University Press, 1961), pp. 504ff.
24. There is no strict incompatibility; only a logical oddity.

*in*formality—unless supplemented by the very symboliza-
tion whose upshot philosophy may then upbraid or still be-
rate.

A perfect and appropriate illustration of the uselessness of
trying to "follow" the alleged dictates of logic *in philosophy*
is given by Quine, inadvertently, in his topical discussion of
elimination of singular terms.[25] Significantly, in the climate
of current intellectual opinion this slick maneuver was
warmly praised rather than roundly condemned as an irrelevant dodging measure, by Quine's otherwise intransi-
gent philosophic opponent, Strawson, in *Individuals* (1959).
Quine, being a hidebound "nominalist" of ancient and ven-
erable standing, did not even wish to grant that individuals
do "exist," startling as this news may sound. But we must
remember to recite Quine's astonishing yet unconsciously
ethical stricture that "there are no ultimate philosophical
problems concerning existence except insofar as existence is
expressed by the quantifier '(∃x).' "[26] Strangely, this reduc-
tionist stand is the only thing that saved Quine from lunacy,
given the extremes to which he carried his refusal to admit
concrete instantiations of personhood into his ultimate on-
tology.

The proper answer, both to Quine and to Peirce, Leibnitz, and the rest, is really the discovery of combinatory
logic by Schoenfinkel, recorded in a paper first published in
1924.[27] According to developments in this branch of
mathematics, *all* variables (including terms, connectives,
and the entire apparatus of, say, first-order quantification

25. W. V. O. Quine, *Methods of Logic*, 2d ed. (New York: Holt, Rinehart and
Winston, 1959), pp. 220ff.

26. *Ibid.*, p. 224. This is as gross a piece of philosophic legislation as the recent
literature can possibly exhibit. Need one wonder what other philosophers concerned with problems of "existence" (Heidegger, Jaspers, Sartre, or even
Whitehead) might say in reply? For further discussion of the unwarranted arrogance indicated by claims of this type, see my paper "The Language of
Philosophy," *Dialectica* 26 (1972): 293-99.

27. M. Schoenfinkel, "On the Building Blocks of Mathematical Logic," translated in J. van Heijenoort, ed., *From Frege to Goedel*, pp. 357-66.

theory) can be resolutely replaced by at most three "operators," which systematically perform all of the functions normally handled by quantifiers, horseshoes, tildes, etcetera. This is logic stripped to its barest. It represents complete austerity. We subsequently learn, principally from the work of Curry,[28] that combinatory logic can be axiomatized, and can be treated set-theoretically, as well as *via* the technique of Goedel numbering, but in none of these guises does logic bear any resemblance to the tool wherewith we used to sort out good (or valid) arguments from bad (or invalid) ones. Combinatory logic cannot be converted into a natural deduction system, nor can it be used to test inferences. In short, it is philosophically *worthless*, except for two purposes: (1) it shows us what logic truly *is*, at its nub; (2) it enables us to undermine and refute Quine (and others) who would advise how salutary the study of logic is, while proceeding to offer pungent recommendations on how we should conduct ourselves accordingly, as philosophers.[29] For, if "to be is to be a value of a variable," as Quine has been telling us consistently since 1939,[30] and if, furthermore, there "are" *no* variables, as combinatory logic shows, then *all* of our "ontological commitments" disappear, or vanish into thin air. Thus, Quine and Heidegger may yet agree that Nothing is,[31] alike disagreeing with Parmenides into the bargain.

28. These results are summarized in H. B. Curry and R. Feys, *Combinatory Logic*, vol. I (Amsterdam: North Holland Publishing, 1958).

29. See in this connection C. S. Peirce, *Collected Papers of Charles Sanders Peirce*, ed. C. Hartshorne and P. Weiss, vol. 1 (Cambridge, Mass.: Harvard University Press, 1931), para. 672 (1.672).

30. W. V. O. Quine, "Designation and Existence," *Journal of Philosophy* 36 (1939): 701-8; *Methods of Logic*, 2d ed., p. 224.

31. Quine does devote an essay, written in 1960, to combinatory logic, but it is singularly impressive in its avoidance of "ontological" issues raised—that is, those which threaten the retention of the Quinean program. See *Selected Logic Papers* (New York: Random House, 1966), pp. 227ff. For some cogent criticism of this position, see H. B. Curry, "The Elimination of Variables by Regular Combinators," in Mario Bunge, ed., *The Critical Approach to Science and Philosophy* (Glencoe, Ill.: Free Press, 1964), pp. 127-43.

Philosophers should take the claims of logic less seriously, at least from now on. No amount of dialectical finesse or logical trickery should produce the active conviction that relations are less than real, that they deserve no status in our thought and vocabulary. The sophistical sleight-of-hand that has been perpetrated with respect to relations will no longer baffle anyone if philosophers learn, slowly and painfully, to dissociate themselves from logic, *both* as an idol of the tribe formerly obeyed slavishly, and as an ogre, to be rebutted at all costs—which means, by taking the high road to wild and fanciful metaphysical obscurantism at worst, or to timid bouts at "clarification" of the issue at best. Disengagement is always preferable to idiocy as a matter of policy, and its impeccable credentials are further supported by noting the deviousness with which philosophers often subject tangible results derived from the discipline of logic to unmerited criticism, whenever confrontation becomes so desperate that it seemingly warrants handing out a license to engage in sophistry.

3. *The Question of Formalism.* At the present time, the drive toward formalism suffers from several handicaps. Because it is associated with the now-discarded Hilbertian (finitistic) program, which eschewed semantics in favor of a rigorous axiomatic development, it is in disrepute among logicians; moreover, its own sympathizers add to the confusion by their rhetorical ineptness. Thus, we find spokesmen (e.g., Barker) on behalf of formalism elaborating a "game-theory" of mathematics, and getting promptly rebuked by philosophers for failing to take their own enterprise to heart. In my opinion, the attempt to compare logic to a "game" is both misleading and dangerous.[32] The term "game" is very poorly chosen; it leaves many people with

---

32. I do not include under this heading the more complicated theories of the late Wittgenstein, which form a topic unto themselves, ideas not to be dismissed lightly. See *Remarks on the Foundations of Mathematics*, trans. G. E. M. Anscombe (Cambridge, Mass.: MIT Press, 1967).

the impression that mathematics involves no cognition, and that it requires neither talent, industry, nor even sobriety in order to master the field. Logic, whatever it is, is not a sport, for in sports not everyone tries to play by the rules! Nor is logic competitive; no one wins or loses at it. And so on, with mounting dissimilarities. On the other hand, logic, if it is a game, is a deadly serious one—not at all the frivolity that the idea of "gamesmanship" or "playing games" connotes. If in the end the truths of logic are, as Locke suggested, "trifling," they are nonetheless anything but trivial in the amount of exertion called forth to establish them.

With so few champions of it who understand formalism from inside, it is not surprising that the literature reveals a dearth of intelligent exposition of its principal features. Among the older generation of formalists, only the monograph composed by Curry[33] stands out; among today's formalist programs will be unnecessary, hence superfluous, cations of the Skolem-Loewenheim theorem, and by the accompanying growth of interest in nonstandard analysis, thanks to the late A. Robinson.

Curry's device of radical usage, as described earlier, is a good example of the primary motives that underlie any urge to adopt the formalist platform. There is a deliberate effort to eschew "entangling ontological alliances," not due to fear of what may come of it philosophically (Quine), but simply for the sake of sharply separating philosophical from mathematical issues, freeing the latter from all the encumbrances, inhibitions, and restraints brought about by prolonged reflection on the former. In the context of disputes over set theory, this is what E. Mendelson reputedly called that "anything goes" policy. In practice what this means is: develop logical systems first, and ask interpretive questions later, if at all.

33. H. B. Curry, *Outlines of a Formalist Philosophy of Mathematics* (Amsterdam: North Holland Publishing, 1951; reprinted 1963).

Oddly, one effect of this policy is unintentionally to promote a return to the ideal of syntax study advocated by Hilbert several decades ago. For instance, anyone who now reads Martin's monograph on pragmatics[34] must be impressed by the narrow and sheerly *syntactical* way in which the entire subject is built up. Add to this the "nominalistic" consideration that, as Quine and Goodman proved in 1947,[35] all that we call semantical in nature can be effectively handled from a purely syntactic point of view,[36] and one can only begin to wonder in what direction formalism is heading, if not retreat into an area where additional formalist programs will be unnecessary, hence superfluous, since all matters of interpretation will already be ruled out, banished, or simply not allowed to arise. If formalism is successful, it eventually must legislate itself out of a useful existence. Regrettably, the same is true of the most recent metamathematical stress on "semantics," which is nothing if not purely syntactical in *its* orientation and actual development.

This is what comes from paying no attention to philosophy; whereas, as I already indicated earlier, what genuine philosophers should do is pay no attention to formal logic; logic, where, as Dewey and Bentley dramatically showed,[37] symbol-manipulation is nothing if not clear,

---

34. R. M. Martin, *Toward a Systematic Pragmatics* (Amsterdam: North Holland Publishing, 1959). Martin's subsequent books, inspired largely by a Quinean conception of logic, have only further articulated and refined some of the basic ideas set forth in this early treatise.

35. W. V. O. Quine and N. Goodman, "Steps Toward a Constructive Nominalism," *Journal of Symbolic Logic* 12 (1947): 105-22.

36. I follow the usual definitions, according to which *syntax* refers strictly to the relationship(s) obtaining between and among signs, *semantics* to the interpreted relations between signs and objects, where "objects" is broadly conceived to include abstractions of all kinds, and *pragmatics* to the relations between signs and interpretants. So construed, semantics is inclusive of syntax, while pragmatics embraces each of the other two; correspondingly, syntax is the narrowest of the three in its extent.

37. A. Bentley and J. Dewey, *Knowing and the Known* (Boston: Beacon Press, 1949).

while the supposedly underlying concepts and purposes seem hopelessly muddled. However, I staunchly maintain that logic and philosophy ought to be kept at a distance, allowing each side to pursue its own course independently. For reasons just propounded, the impetus for such a move ought initially to come from philosophy, not from logic. This is quite apart from arguments based on the most obvious truth of all, namely, that syntax for syntax's sake can only yield the most arid and meaningless results, as all of research work demonstrates convincingly, through the setting of a prominent, dismal, and unhappy example. So the entire formalist enterprise begins as it ends, in barrenness, no matter under whose banner (syntax, semantics, or pragmatics) it is nominally flown.

No better or more clinching illustration of the utter failure of formalism, whether measured by philosophy or by its own standards, can be had than by looking up the definition of truth proposed by A. Tarski, in his most famous work:[38]

Def. x is a true sentence—in symbols $x \in Tr$—iff $x \in S$ and every infinite sequence of classes satisfies x.

This definition is just a formal reconstruction, endowed, to be sure, with the modern apparatus of sets and classes, of that originally offered near the beginning of Western metaphysics by Aristotle.[39] And yet, it is widely recognized that Tarski's definition is open to all of the following sorts of objections: (a) philosophically trivial ('S' is true if and only if S); (b) neutral with respect to competing or rival philosophic "theories" of truth; (c) merely relative to some language, an artificially constructed one, at that.

All this does not yet charge Tarski's theory with totally

---

38. A. Tarski, *Logic, Semantics, Metamathematics*, trans. J. H. Woodger (Oxford: Clarendon Press, 1956), pp. 155 n2, 187-88, 195.
39. Aristotle, *Metaphysics*, 4.1011b 26-28.

lacking merit. As K. Popper observes, on many fronts it does enable science to go forward, unimpeded by irritating "foundational" issues, irritating because hitherto unsettled. And, as M. Black and others have claimed from time to time, its very vices can be made out to be, or else made over into, virtues: its philosophic obviousness is welcome, and becomingly unproblematic in an area infested by insuperable difficulties at every stage of inquiry; while its alleged triviality frees it from the kind of deeper objections that might otherwise be lodged against it. Its lack of differential content with respect to the war still being fought out among adherents to correspondence, coherence, and pragmatic viewpoints, respectively, renders it supremely adaptable, either as an instrument for temporarily overcoming division, or else as a standing partner, one that is forever compatible with (and acceptable to) the ultimate philosophic victor in *that* battle, no matter what its future identity should turn out to be. Finally, that it rests on a mere "convention" means that a (if not *the)* language for discussing the problem of truth has been found (by inventing one!), a language where we as philosophers shall be able to control both the vocabulary and the rules-for-use from the outset, instead of being prey to mesmerism and torture, owing to the delusions by which one is so often victimized in carelessly employing ordinary discourse in technical matters.[40]

However, the chief difficulty facing Tarski, or formalists in general, is not based upon such considerations as those just adduced. Rather, it rests upon the utter superficiality of the concept of truth as it is dealt with from beginning to end. Whether with respect to its meaning or its denotation,

---

40. One thinks of Heidegger's acrobatic feats with Greek etymologies; or, negatively, of Ryle's quip that he is not opposing "ordinary" to technical language, but only to extraordinary language. Frequently, however, the two (or the three) merge, as when they are combined in twaddlesome philosophic discourse!

one cannot imagine Tarski offering his definition of truth-in-L in reply to Pilate's question. Can you?

In short, the problem of Truth has not even been touched. Deep issues have been left aside, in favor of an easy, convenient, but ultimately self-deceptive brand of symbol-mongering. Not only is the formulation philosophically trivial, it is of no help in trying to do something, however modest or humble, about those philosophically inescapable problems of life, whether "life" be given small or capital letters. Tarski and his followers, no less than his analytically inclined detractors, have nothing, nothing of value, to say to *men*. They have neither explored nor exploited Truth, but merely debased and degraded it. While it is definitely the business of the philosopher to unearth a consistent meaning out of such notions as necessity and possibility, the formalist logician takes a costly shortcut to understanding, by detaching himself from the world—and for what? To fool and, yes, "play" with the square and diamond operators. Harmless as manipulating these logical operators is as a mere activity, when and if the logician finally gets around to interpretation of their significance, it is small wonder that he faces grave trouble. The recent history of modal logic affords ample testimony of this (not to mention futile applications to the sphere of ethics, in formal deontology, as erected by von Wright *et al.*)

The philosopher justifiably may, and indeed should, neglect symbolic logic, whereas the logician ignores both philosophy and life at his own peril. Ever since Bertrand Russell, however, prevailing sentiment in philosophy itself has tended to instruct just the opposite bias. But, as the issue of Truth alone finally ought to show us, if nothing else will, it is high time that we in philosophy reversed this anti-human moral. Should the flow of change again be in a more philosophical direction, discursive, dialectical thought will at last enjoy unparalleled, unprecedented triumph over the collective forces of pro-syntax. It will then amount to a hard-earned intellectual victory, a successful "political" struggle, and one long overdue. My purpose here has been to help make a large and persuasive opening contribution to reaching that end.

Appendix
to Chapter 6

O ne of the conclusions I have come to in examining the
teaching habits of logicians is that they tend to promote a highly technical context both for themselves and for
their students. This results in a conspicuous lack of concrete
applications, which further aggravates the already hard job
of getting logic across to nonlogicians (philosophers and
non-philosophers alike). Such a vicious pedagogical circle
must be broken into somewhere, and in this appendix I
wish to make a start.

Consider only the use-mention distinction in this connection. In footnote 10 of this chapter, I adduced a possible or

imaginary case in which use-mention was not heeded, thus resulting in marital disharmony of sorts. But this was light-hearted and improbable. Consider instead something actual and far more grave: a 1963 Supreme Court ruling with reference to prayer in the public schools. It seems that in one state school district, the principal of a certain institution attempted an artful dodge of the 1963 ban by reading the *Congressional Record* at each auditorium session. He was promptly sued by irate parents, and thus the matter was brought before the bar.[1]

Naturally, the principal defended himself by arguing that he was merely quoting Congress. But the Justices saw through this ruse of indirection, and, with a less feeling eye for use and mention, forbade the practice of conducting religious prayers through the medium of political minute-taking,[2] by *oratio obliqua* no less!

Here was a vital instance in which use *vs.* mention not only came up, but was put to the test, legally and morally. Yet one finds no "mention" of this in logic textbooks or classrooms, which is all too typical and desultory. It is relatively unimportant (although highly consequential for the parties invovled) whether the Supreme Court's decision can be cited as "evidence" in favor of eradicating altogether the use-mention distinction, on which the principal briefly throve. I have already claimed on other grounds that a modification may be in order.

What is at stake here is the vivification of an otherwise dead husk, desirable for the sake of teaching the subject if

1. Each session of Congress is preceded by a Bible-reading or similar religious invocation, and as it happens, the full text is inserted at the head of the complete log for the day, and then printed up. The basis of the lawsuit was twofold: (1) unconstitutionality; (2) infringement or denial of civil rights, as guaranteed both to the parents or guardians and to their offspring.

2. The principal would appear to have taken his cues from A. Church, since he was both using (reading) and mentioning (quoting from, in indirect discourse) the Scriptures, simultaneously.

for no other reason. It is no wonder that even a "glamorous" topic such as recursive function theory is much harder to grasp for lack of producing some tangible relation to an actual state of affairs, one that is realizable (preferably) in the everyday world of men and events, and their mutual surroundings.[3] Without this tangible matrix, logic might as well go up in smoke as make any concrete sense. Of course, my plea has a Deweyan ring (borrowing, in fact, from his last public lecture, delivered in 1947). But it is better to lean upon the views of Dewey for support, as I did at the very outset of this chapter, than to try the futile expedient of justifying logic in any number of disappointing ways that rely or trade upon the methods that I have already exposed (and subsequently decried) as worthless ploys, and that enjoy such tremendous (and undeserved) popularity at the present time.

3. In the case of mathematical induction, an equally astute (and philosophically direct) procedure could involve comparison with the basic assumptions or presuppositions of the movment known as "logical atomism"—an analogy that, so far as I know, has gone entirely unnoticed.

Selective Bibliography

This list includes all important works cited in the text or notes, together with some additional writings of significance for the reader interested in pursuing further the themes and interpretations of this book. Titles are restricted to works available in the English language; editions that are easily accessible have been chosen.

Aristotle. *The Basic Works of Aristotle*. Translation "Oxford edition." Edited by R. P. McKeon. New York: Random House, 1941.

Augustine, St. *Confessions*. Translated by R. S. Pine-Coffin. Baltimore: Penguin Books, 1961.

Austin, J. L. *Philosophical Papers*. Edited by J. O. Urmson and G. J. Warnock. Oxford: Clarendon Press, 1961; 2nd ed., 1970.

Ballard, E. G. *Socratic Ignorance.* The Hague: Martinus Nijhoff, 1968.

Berlin, I. *The Hedgehog and the Fox.* New York: Simon & Schuster, 1953.

Blanshard, B. "Kierkegaard on Faith." *The Personalist* 49 (1968): 5-23.

Bouwsma, O. K. *Philosophical Essays.* Lincoln, Neb.: University of Nebraska Press, 1965.

Brumbaugh, R. S. *Plato for the Modern Age.* New York: Collier, 1962.

Carnap, R. *The Logical Structure of the World and Pseudoproblems in Philosophy.* Translated by R. A. George. Berkeley and Los Angeles: University of California Press, 1967.

Caton, C. E., ed. *Philosophy and Ordinary Language.* Urbana, Ill.: University of Illinois Press, 1963.

Church, A. *Introduction to Mathematical Logic,* vol. 1. Princeton, N.J.: Princeton University Press, 1956.

Cleve, F. M. *The Giants of Pre-Sophistic Greek Philosophy.* 2 vols. The Hague: Martinus Nijhoff, 1965.

Curry, H. B. *Outlines of a Formalist Philosophy of Mathematics.* Amsterdam: North Holland Publishing, 1951; reprinted 1963.

Descartes, R. *The Philosophical Works of Descartes.* Translated by E. S. Haldane and G. R. T. Ross. 2 vols. Cambridge: Cambridge University Press, 1911; reprinted 1931, 1955.

Dewey, J. *Experience and Nature.* 2nd ed. Chicago: Open Court, 1929.

———. *Logic: The Theory of Inquiry.* New York: Holt, 1938.

———. *The Quest for Certainty.* New York: G. P. Putnam's, 1929; reprinted 1960.

Donnelly, J. "Re-examining Kierkegaard's 'Teleological Suspension of the Ethical.' " In J. Donnelly, ed., *Logical Analysis and Contemporary Theism.* New York: Fordham University Press, 1972. Pp. 294-331.

Edwards, P. "Kierkegaard and the 'Truth' of Christianity." *Philosophy* 46 (1971): 89-108.

Flew, A. G. N. *An Introduction to Western Philosophy: Ideas and Argument from Plato to Sartre.* Indianapolis, Ind.: Bobbs-Merrill, 1971.

Garelick, H. *The Anti-Christianity of Kierkegaard.* The Hague: Martinus Nijhoff, 1965.

Gilson, E. *History of Christian Philosophy in the Middle Ages*. New York: Random House, 1955.

Gulley, N. *The Philosophy of Socrates*. London: Methuen, 1968.

Guthrie, W. K. C. *A History of Greek Philosophy*, vol. 3. Cambridge: Cambridge University Press, 1969. Part II reprinted separately as *Socrates*. Cambridge University Press, 1971.

Hegel, G. W. F. *Phenomenology of Mind*. Translated by J. B. Baillie. New edition, introduction by G. Lichtheim. New York: Harper and Row, 1967.

Heidegger, M. "Who is Nietzsche's Zarathustra?" *Review of Metaphysics* 20 (1967): 411-31.

Hintikka, K. J. J. "*Cogito, ergo sum:* Inference or Performance?" *Philosophical Review* 71 (1962): 3-32; see also 72 (1963): 487-96, for replies to critics.

Holmer, P. L. "Kierkegaard and Logic." *Kierkegaardiana* 2 (1957): 25-42.

Hudson, W. D. *Modern Moral Philosophy*. Garden City, N.Y.: Doubleday, 1970.

Hume, D. *A Treatise of Human Nature*. Edited by L. A. Selby-Bigge. Oxford: Clarendon Press, 1888. (Frequently reprinted.)

―――. *An Inquiry Concerning the Principles of Morals*. Edited by C. W. Hendel. Indianapolis, Ind.: Bobbs-Merrill, 1957.

Kant, I. *Critique of Pure Reason*. Translated by N. Kemp Smith. 2nd ed. London: Macmillan, 1933; reprinted, 1963.

Kaufmann, W. *Nietzsche: Philosopher, Psychologist, Anti-Christ*. 3rd ed. New York: Random House, 1968.

Kierkegaard, S. *Concluding Unscientific Postscript*. Translated by D. F. Swenson and W. Lowrie. Princeton, N.J.: Princeton University Press, 1941.

―――. *Either/Or*. Translated by D. F. Swenson, L. M. Swenson, and W. Lowrie. Revised H. A. Johnson. Princeton, N.J.: Princeton University Press, 1959.

―――. *Fear and Trembling*. Translated by W. Lowrie. Princeton, N.J.: Princeton University Press, 1954.

―――. *Johannes Climacus: or, De Omnibus Dubitandum Est, and a Sermon*. Translated by T. H. Croxall. Stanford, Calif.: Stanford University Press, 1958.

―――. *Philosophical Fragments*. Translated by D. F. Swenson. Commentary N. Thulstrup; revised H. Hong. Princeton, N.J.: Princeton University Press, 1962.

Kneale, W., and Kneale, M. *The Development of Logic.* Oxford: Clarendon Press, 1962.

Lewis, C. I. *A Survey of Symbolic Logic.* Berkeley and Los Angeles: University of California Press, 1918; reprinted 1960.

Linsky, L., ed. *Semantics and the Philosophy of Language.* Urbana, Ill.: University of Illinois Press, 1952; reprinted 1968.

Lovejoy, A. O. *The Great Chain of Being.* Cambridge, Mass.: Harvard University Press, 1936.

Mackey, L. *Kierkegaard: A Kind of Poet.* Philadelphia: University of Pennsylvania Press, 1971.

————. "Philosophy and Poetry in Kierkegaard." *Review of Metaphysics* 23 (1969): 316-32.

Mates, B. *Elementary Logic.* New York: Oxford University Press, 1965.

Mill, J. S. "On Liberty." In J. Stillinger, ed., *Autobiography and Other Writings.* Boston: Houghton Mifflin, 1969. (Also many other editions.)

————. "Utilitarianism." In J. M. Robson, ed., *Essays on Ethics, Religion, and Society* (Mill, *Collected Works,* vol. 10). Toronto: University of Toronto Press, 1969. (Also many other editions.)

Murphey, M. *The Development of Peirce's Philosophy.* Cambridge, Mass.: Harvard University Press, 1961.

Nietzsche, F. *Beyond Good and Evil.* Translated by M. Cowan. Chicago: Regnery, 1955.

————. *The Birth of Tragedy and the Genealogy of Morals.* Translated F. Golffing. Garden City, N.Y.: Doubleday, 1956.

————. "The Antichrist." In *The Portable Nietzsche.* Translated by W. Kaufmann. New York: Random House, 1954.

————. *The Will to Power.* Translated by W. Kaufmann and R. J. Hollingdale. New York: Random House, 1967.

————. *Thus Spoke Zarathustra.* Translated by W. Kaufmann. New York: Viking Press, 1966.

O'Brien, M. J. *The Socratic Paradoxes and the Greek Mind.* Chapel Hill, N.C.: University of North Carolina Press, 1967.

Passmore, J. *A Hundred Years of Philosophy.* Rev. ed. Baltimore: Penguin Books, 1968.

Peirce, C. S. *Collected Papers of Charles Sanders Peirce.* 8 vols. Edited by C. Hartshorne, P. Weiss, A. Burks. Cambridge,

Mass.: Harvard University Press, 1931-35, 1958; reprinted in 4 vols. 1960.

Plato. *Plato: The Collected Dialogues.* Edited by E. Hamilton and H. Cairns. New York: Bollingen Foundation, 1961.

Quine, W. V. O. *Mathematical Logic.* Rev. ed. Cambridge, Mass.: Harvard University Press, 1951.

――――. *Methods of Logic.* 2nd ed. New York: Holt, Rinehart and Winston, 1959.

Randall, J. H., Jr. *Plato: Dramatist of the Life of Reason.* New York: Columbia University Press, 1970.

Ross, J. F. *Philosophical Theology.* Indianapolis, Ind.: Bobbs-Merrill, 1969.

Schrader, G. "Kant and Kierkegaard on Duty and Inclination." *Journal of Philosophy* 65 (1968): 688-701; reprinted in Thompson 1972, *q.v.*, below.

Singer, M. G. "Formal Logic and Dewey's Logic." *Philosophical Review* 60 (1951): 375-85.

Sparshott, F. E. "Socrates and Thrasymachus." *The Monist* 50 (1966): 421-59.

Tarski, A. *Logic, Semantics, Metamathematics.* Translated by J. H. Woodger. Oxford: Clarendon Press, 1956.

――――. "The Semantic Conception of Truth, and the Foundations of Semantics." *Philosophy and Phenomenological Research* 4 (1944-45): 341-76; reprinted in Linsky, *q.v.*, above.

Taylor, R. "Dare to Be Wise." *Review of Metaphysics* 21 (1967-68): 615-29.

Thompson, J., ed. *Kierkegaard: A Collection of Critical Essays.* Garden City, N.Y.: Doubleday, 1972.

――――. *The Lonely Labyrinth: Kierkegaard's Pseudonymous Corpus, 1843-1846.* Carbondale, Ill.: Southern Illinois University Press, 1967.

Van Heijenoort, J., ed. *From Frege to Goedel: A Source Book in Mathematical Logic, 1879–1931.* Cambridge, Mass.: Harvard University Press, 1967.

Veatch, H. B. *Two Logics.* Evanston, Ill.: Northwestern University Press, 1969.

Walsh, J. J. *Aristotle's Conception of Moral Weakness.* New York and London: Columbia University Press, 1963.

William, of Sherwood. *William of Sherwood's Introduction to Logic.* Minneapolis, Minn.: University of Minnesota Press, 1966.

――――. *William of Sherwood's Treatise on Syncategorematic*

Words. Edited by N. Kretzmann. Minneapolis, Minn.: University of Minnesota Press, 1968.

Wittgenstein, L. *Philosophical Investigations*. Translated by G. E. M. Anscombe. New York: Macmillan, 1953; 3rd ed., 1967.

―――. *Remarks on the Foundations of Mathematics*. Edited by G. H. von Wright, R. Rhees, and G. E. M. Anscombe. Translated by G. E. M. Anscombe. Cambridge, Mass.: MIT Press, 1967.

―――. *Zettel*. Edited by G. E. M. Anscombe and G. H. von Wright. Translated by G. E. M. Anscombe. Berkeley and Los Angeles: University of California Press, 1970.

Wolff, R. P. *The Poverty of Liberalism*. Boston: Beacon Press, 1968.

Index of Names

Index of Special Topics